WHY ME, GOD?

*Understanding the Calling God
Designed for Your Life*

Emily Michael

WHY ME, GOD?

Scripture quotations are taken from the *Holy Bible*,
New Living Translation, copyright ©1996, 2004,
2015 by Tyndale House Foundation. Used by
permission of Tyndale House Publishers, Carol
Stream, Illinois 60188. All rights reserved.

ISBN: 979-8-218-47248-1
First Edition: July 2024

Printed in the United States of America

*To every person striving to walk in
God's calling for their lives.*

CONTENTS

INTRODUCTION

THE ROAD LESS TRAVELED

Let me be honest: There is nothing that qualifies me to write this book. I do not have a background in English. I am not a world-renowned author with exquisite penmanship. I do not have a Theology degree and I have not memorized every verse of the Bible. No fancy title or big platform. I am just like you. A person pursuing a healthy, blessed life. Someone hungry for God and in love with the beautiful life He has planned for me.

So, why am I writing this book? I would like to tell you that I have had a passion for writing my whole life. I would be lying if I said I have had this book trapped inside of me forever and I've been dying to get these words on paper. The truth is, God called me to do this. If I am *completely* honest, I was terrified when I started writing this book!

I did not feel qualified. I did not think my words mattered. I did not really know what to say or why God would call someone like me to write a book in the first place. Why would anyone want to read this? *Why me, God?* There was not a clear understanding of why this was something He needed me to do. All I knew was that God had asked me to do it.

Many of you may be in the same position I found myself in. Whether you are reading this from your desk, the treadmill, or the comfort of your bed, we have all asked the lingering question: *Why me, God?* If you know you have been called by God, you have stumbled across a product for empowerment, and I am here to encourage you to walk into your calling with confidence.

Introduction

There is no easy explanation for why God calls someone to do something. There is no proven or logical reasoning behind why God has placed that specific task in your hands. And I know what you are thinking,

If that is the case, what is the point of this book?

Well, I'll tell you. Your calling is designed for you and only you. The people you connect with, your career, and everything in between. It's a call to help reach the lost. To help those who don't know God find Him. With that being said, you can have a calling on your life and disqualify yourself based on what you do not know or understand. In other words, you will miss what God has for you because it does not make sense.

*Why would God ask me to do this? I
don't even know where to start!*

Rest assured; you are right where
you need to be. God doesn't call people
to what they feel qualified to do, but He
does qualify you to fulfill your calling.
Do you think Noah felt qualified to
build an ark that would hold two of
every animal and withstand flood
waters sent by God? Do you think
Moses felt qualified to lead the
Israelites out of Egypt to the promised
land? How about Mary when the angel
told her she would give birth to the Son
of God? Do you think she felt qualified
to raise the Savior of the World?
Probably not.

It's not your feelings or credentials that
matter. It's not about having all the answers
or having total and complete knowledge of

every detail of the assignment. You won't always understand God's calling for your life, and you're not meant to. If God told you everything you would go through, you would never walk in the calling He designed for you. This life with God is not easy. It does not make you exempt from experiencing pain or hardship. As a matter of fact, Jesus told us, "I have told you all this so that you may have peace in me. Here on earth you will have many trials and sorrows. But take heart, because I have overcome the world." (John 16:33, NLT)

He wanted us to know that there is still pain, regardless of whether or not you believe in God. He also wanted us to know that no matter what we go through in life, we can find comfort in Him. It's not about the calling, it's about your "yes" to the call, and how it will impact the kingdom of God. Answering the call is not for the weak. It will take sacrifice, discipline, and strength like you've never known before. Let's call it… taking *the road less traveled.*

This is the part no one likes to hear, but I'm happy to deliver the bad news: Your calling is not about you. That's right. Your calling uses you, it is for you, but it is not about you. God *chose* you. He chose to use you. God will ask you to give things up. He will give you instructions designed for your calling. There will be people you can't talk to, places you can't go to, and old hobbies given up for new hobbies. He may even tell you to stop eating your favorite snacks (bye bye, fudge brownies).

But let's not get ahead of ourselves. This isn't meant to scare you; it's meant to prepare you. Every person has a purpose, but only a few will truly accomplish all God has set out for them. And let me give you some comfort, God is with you. The fact that

Introduction

He called you should be proof enough.
Psalm 37:23 NLT says, "The Lord directs
the steps of the godly. He delights in every
detail of their lives." God cares for you.
That's why He called you. He's not leaving
you to figure it out, He's guiding you every
step of the way.

Remember, you're reading these words
from an "unqualified" vessel. Nothing could
have qualified me for this, only God. The
reason this book exists is out of my "yes" to
the call. And don't write off your calling
based on your interpretation of its
significance. Every calling has value.
Whether you've been called to start a
nonprofit to feed the homeless or your
calling leads you to work in ministry. Your
calling could even be serving your family in
the manner God has asked you to.

Each and every calling is equally
important to God as it's designed

specifically for you. I pray as you continue reading, you find new strength to trust God in the unknown. To walk confidently and boldly into your calling. Let this be a resource to help you understand its value. We're all in this together. The real question you must ask yourself now is, "Are you ready to take *the road less traveled*?"

CHAPTER 1

ACCEPTING THE CALL

In today's world, having a phone is a necessity. It's one of the first things you grab when you wake up in the morning. Your phone is on the checklist of items you make sure you have as you scramble to get out the door: *phone, wallet, keys*. It is rare that someone does not have a phone with them. It doesn't matter where they are going or what they are doing, people want to make sure they have their phone with them at all times. But it wasn't that long ago that phones were not accessible to us at every minute of the day.

Only in the last 50 years have we been able to have access to portable phones. What we know as cell phones. However, phones started as landlines. If you don't know what a landline is, and I'm sure I'm aging myself here, it is a phone that plugs into the wall for connection so that your home can receive phone calls. Landlines do not have the same capabilities our cell phones do.

Right now, if I wanted to conference call multiple people in different countries around the world, I could do that through an app on my cellular device. Through a landline, you were lucky to have a phone call that kept a stable connection clear enough to understand what the person on the other line was saying to you, though I'm sure they've improved since my childhood. When phones were first invented, there was no access to caller ID, so you had no way of knowing who was calling and for what reason. Text messaging and voicemail were not a thing. That's what mailing a letter was for. When you called someone, you hoped they would answer, and if they didn't, you'd have to call them back later. And do not get me started on answering machines.

We have come a long way from plastic phones with a spinning number dial. No more having to hold a curved cylinder to our ears to hear and speak to someone while twirling the spiral chord it is connected to. Oh, how times have changed! In some ways, these changes have been good for us. Having a phone with you at all times ensures that you can be contacted when needed. If an emergency arises, you have the ability to call someone for help. You can stay continuously working and busy because most phones function in more ways than just for calling or messaging.

On the other hand, the evolution of our phones can be seen in a negative way. Always being accessible is not necessarily a good thing. Consistently being on our phones, we miss a lot of what is going on around us. This also makes connecting with people less personable as it is easier for us to just send a text or give them a quick call to chat. Lately, I have found myself struggling to even do that as I have felt the constant pull towards my phone being exhausting. If you are anything like me, you almost feel desensitized to communication.

As a society, we have the most access to people, and yet, we have never been more disconnected. Every hang out must be followed by a picture posted on social media, or it is like it didn't happen. Commenting on someone's post is more important than checking in with your friends via text or phone call. Most conversations revolve around sending videos or memes we can relate to rather than having deep and meaningful talks. We don't even remember phone numbers or birthdays anymore, just plug the numbers into our phone and it saves everything. If someone calls you, it should be work related or urgent, otherwise, it could have been a text. We are less likely to answer a phone call now than we have ever been.

The distance between personal relationships is something God never wanted for us. In fact, He created us to do life together. Not by phone, but by community, conversations, and genuine connections. It's not just how He wanted us to have relationships with one another, it's how He designed us to have relationship with Him. God created us to experience life with Him in a personal way. He wants to walk with us daily, talk with us daily, guide our paths, and lead us through life. God does this in a way that is familiar to us: He calls us.

Now, God doesn't physically pick up a phone and ring you up. When God calls you,

He is pulling you towards His plan for your life. His plan helps you walk in purpose. The calling God has for you directly correlates to your life experiences, gifts and skills, and your willingness to be used by Him. That last part is where we will start. Your calling can only be known by God. In order for you to be able to receive God's calling, you have to be readily available to Him. God knows you. After all, He created you! But it's not enough for Him to know you, you need to know Him.

Have you ever had someone call you that you have never known a day in your life? When was the last time you accepted a call from someone you did not know? Exactly. And when you do, think about how awkward those calls usually are. *"Umm, sorry, who are you and why are you calling me?"* If you're anything like me, you try to end that call as soon as possible. Why would you want to talk to someone you do not know? So, I have some questions for you:

- How well do you know God?
- Do you know God's voice?
- Would you recognize God's voice if He was speaking to you right now?
- If I asked you what you know about God, what would your response be?
- Who is God to you?

Before you can even think about accepting your calling from the Lord, you need to know Him. How can we come to know God? Great question! The 3 most important ways you can grow your knowledge of God are:

1.) Reading the Bible
2.) Spending time in His presence
3.) Prayer

The Bible is the written word of God. This is your guide to understanding what God has done, what He is currently doing, and what He will do. God outlines and explains every important part of history. From how the Earth began to our redemption through Jesus Christ dying on the cross for our salvation. God gives us instructions for how we should live our lives right now and how we can be connected to Him. God details what the future holds through the book of Revelation. There are a multitude of scriptures explaining God and His character.

The more time you spend in the Bible, the more you will learn about God and open your heart for God to reveal himself to you in new ways. The Bible is the only book in this world that can personally transform you from the inside out, if you let it of course. This is our guide to understanding and living with God. Without knowledge of the word, we will struggle to live our lives for God and walk as He directs us to.

Another way to grow your relationship with God is by spending time in His presence. That might sound strange as God is not visible to us. How can you spend time with someone you cannot see? By His spirit. We are spiritual beings in human flesh. Spiritual beings made in God's image. The spirit that dwells in us comes from God. We are directly connected to God through spirit. If you make time for God, He will show up.

The most common way to spend time in God's presence is through worship. Whether you are singing and dancing to worship music, journaling, or even meditating on the word. If you open your heart, God will meet you right where you are. I can tell you from personal experience there is nothing like sitting in the presence of God. Over the years, the way I have spent time in His presence has evolved as my relationship with Him has gone deeper. You will find that the more you spend time with God, the more He will draw you to see Him in new ways.

Finally, prayer is our most powerful tool. As human beings, prayer is our direct connection to speak with God. There is the power of life and death in our tongue. What you say matters! As you pray, you unlock doors and open heaven by tapping into your undeserved privilege of being an heir to the kingdom of God. We have this power because of Jesus Christ.

When we pray, we are acknowledging God's presence and authority over our lives. We are giving God full access to what we pray over, which allows Him to move in ways we cannot see. We are pursuing God through faith, which is confidence in what we are hoping for and assurance about what we don't currently see (Hebrews 11:1 NLT). All while acknowledging the good things He has already done. Prayer changes everything and it allows us to stay connected to God.

As you develop a deeper relationship with God, you will start to build trust in Him. As you build trust in God, it will unlock His ability to walk with you. Walking with God, you will find that He has a plan for your life. He wants to guide your steps and lead you towards the things He planned for you long ago. These plans are known as your calling. God has a calling for each and every one of us. Our calling is designed specifically for us. He not only wants to reveal His calling for your life to you, but He wants you to trust Him enough to accept it. God will never force you to choose Him. The more you seek Him, the more you will find that He does all things for the love of His children.

God loved us so much that He gave us salvation through Jesus Christ so we could have the option of a life with Him. Yes, you read that right. The keyword in that sentence is *option*. We decide whether or not we want God. It's a choice. Just like our choice to be connected to our families or friends, we can choose to live this life with God or be away from Him. God gave us free will. However, the choice you make will come with stipulations.

If you choose a life with God, you are choosing to lay down your life for His plans. You are choosing to pick up your cross and carry it daily. Your life is no longer your own, it is His. You are choosing a life of sacrifice. But if you choose to be away from Him, you choose the consequence of having to go through life as the world does. You will be compromised. Now, sacrifice and compromise have similar connotations, but there's a distinction between the two.

When you sacrifice something, you are giving up what you desire for something better. This is an act done in love. When you compromise something, you are giving in to something for the sake of agreement. This is an act done in selfishness. Compromise allows you to maintain a certain level of control over your decision to agree. It's much more comfortable to compromise, whereas sacrifice requires you to give up your wants, relinquishing control. Living for God means sacrificing your plans for His.

We must never forget this world is temporary. To compromise ourselves on earth is to forfeit our eternity in heaven. "You can enter God's Kingdom only through the narrow gate. The highway to hell is broad, and its gate is wide for the many who choose that way. But the gateway to life is very narrow and the road is difficult, and only a few ever find it." (Matthew 7:13-14 NLT). Why do you think this is? I'll tell you. It's because of compromise. A life of compromise is a life of selfishness. It's choosing to live how you want to and ignoring God's plans for you.

No matter how much good you do on this earth, it will never be enough to get you into heaven. Why? Heaven was designed for us to live life with God after our life is done here on earth. If we don't choose God on earth, how can God expect us to choose Him in heaven? Especially when we have knowledge of who He is right now but choose to compromise ourselves for the world and our own comfort or pleasure.

Your decision to sacrifice your life for the life God has for you is the beginning of forever. When God reveals your calling, if you choose to accept it, it is the start of the rest of your life. Physically and spiritually. It is a choice to allow God to lead you and have faith that He knows what's best for you. What your calling comes down to is faith. Faith is your ability to trust God. By developing a relationship with God and learning to trust Him more, you demonstrate faith in the acceptance of your calling and sacrifice of your will for His.

Are you ready to walk in the calling God designed for your life? If so, welcome to the beginning of eternity! As we walk through understanding our calling and its value, I want you to remember one thing: God loves you. He designed you intentionally. He knew you before you were born. His calling for your life is yours and yours alone. No one has the same calling as you. No one in this world is like you. You are special to God and He loves you dearly.

Accepting God's call for your life is the starting line. Now that we've warmed up, let's get ready to start running our race. We have a long way to go!

CHAPTER 2

THE FIRST STEP

Everyone with a cell phone has experienced the moment when your screen lights up with an incoming call. Depending on who is calling, the feeling of answering the call can be one of excitement, frustration, annoyance, sadness. A range of emotions can rush through us as we prepare to answer the incoming call or ignore it completely. Sometimes we don't want to answer because we don't know who or what is on the other line. Other times, life gets the best of us and the thought of answering the call can feel heavy.

Your calling from God is exactly the same. There is so much pressure to be joyful and gladly answer every call from God, but if we are honest, there are times we feel God calling us to people, places, and things we really do not want to be the answer to. It could be a person who hurt you, a place that was traumatic, or working a job you have no prior experience in. It could even be connecting or reconnecting with family you have not spoken to in years. There are many ways God can call us. If we are completely honest, some of those calls we want to immediately decline or let them go to voicemail.

"God, I will check on this later."
"God, it is not time yet."
"God, I will do this when I am ready."

If you are anything like me, you sit and contemplate answering the call, going over every thought in your brain.

The First Step

"I do not know if I am ready for this
yet."
"God, are you sure? Like REALLY
sure?!"
"What if this fails and everything falls
apart?"

Or we do the worst thing we could possibly do… turn on airplane mode. But let's not get ahead of ourselves, we will dive into this later.

Here is the thing about receiving a call: when a call comes in, you only have so much time to answer it. When God calls you, it is no different. Your calling has an expiration date. Think about it: Noah only had so much time to build the ark before God flooded the earth. Though an exact time is not written in scripture, Noah grew in age every day that he worked on the calling God placed on him. He was 600 years old when God flooded the earth (Genesis 7:6).

Now, I don't know about you, but I am barely hitting my thirties and I struggle to get out of bed in the morning. Could you imagine God asking you to build an ark, telling you He was going to flood the earth and everyone would die except you, your family, and a bunch of animals because the ark would protect you? Talk about a *heavy* call.

You don't see a Bible verse in the old testament that says, "And God told Noah, 'Take your time getting the ark ready, no rush, I will wait for you and do it on your time, friend." Absolutely not. As a matter of fact, the Bible tells us in Genesis 6 how God gave Noah specific instructions for the ark, explaining why it needed to be built, what type of wood to use, how to keep it sustained through the flood, exact measurements for how large the boat would be, and even how many of each animal would inhabit the boat.

All of these details are important for the calling God placed on Noah, but my favorite part of this story comes after the instructions. The Bible says, "So Noah did everything exactly as God had commanded him." (Genesis 6:22 NLT). One sentence to explain how we should answer every call from God - with obedience. Not delayed obedience. Not prolonged obedience. Not hesitated obedience. Just obedience.

You will not find a part of this story saying, "And Noah decided he would take a few months off because building an ark is hard work." No, instead, Noah got the call and went straight to work. This is the example we should refer to when we answer a call from God. But that's just it, you have to accept the call.

If you have to accept the call first, then why is the title of this chapter 'The First Step?' Seems a little out of order.

The answer is simple: you cannot step into something you have not accepted. Have you ever seen a runner participate in a race they did not sign up or train for? I did not think so. Accepting the call is where we start. God gives us the details and we decide whether or not this is something we are going to do. It's our starting point. We have a choice to run this race or not.

If Noah had told God "Yeah, see, this is a pretty big thing you want me to do and I am not really ready to take this on. I cannot accept at THIS time, but check back next year," could you imagine how different things would be? It is important to understand that accepting the call happens

before you take the first step into your
calling.

OBEDIENCE

As a young girl, I was carefree and
ready for adventure. I wanted to play all the
games, sing every song, and dance until my
little legs could not take it anymore! I was
always on the go and did not want to be
stopped! My mom worked day and night.
When she was not at work, she was taking
online classes trying to further her education
to give us a better life. I was one of five
children, and I would say I was, and still am,
the sassiest. One day, my mom asked me to
clean my room. I think you all know where
this is going.

Why Me, God?

"You are not to do another thing until
this room is cleaned up!"

I did not want to clean! Did my mom
not realize I just wanted to live my life?
Who cares that my room is messy?! I don't
and I live in it! There was another girl close
to my age who lived next door. She had all
the cool toys, and I was trying to go play
with her and whip up a sweet meal in that
awesome toy kitchen she had. This was
much more important than cleaning my
room. At least that is what I thought.

I asked my mom if I could go next door
to play and I bet you could guess what her
response was…

"Did you clean your room yet?"

C'mon, mom! Chef Emily has
customers waiting! You're ruining my life!

The First Step

As you can imagine, she sent me to my room, where I was to remain until it was cleaned. Laying on the bed, I couldn't help but feel upset. I stared at the ceiling for what felt like hours, until I finally decided to start cleaning. After all, my room was dirty, and if I had to sit in here, I might as well do something.

The truth is I loved cleaning. That sounds unreal for a little girl on the go, but it is true. Rearranging and organizing gave my room its own little personality. It helped me maintain some form of individuality in a house full of siblings. It was my safe space. Once I finished cleaning my room, I wanted to show my mom! I was so excited with how good it looked and how I did it all by myself. Nevermind the fact that I threw a fit about cleaning it, that was in the past. This clean room meant so much to me now.

Why Me, God?

After my mom checked to make sure everything was *actually* clean (nothing under the bed or thrown in the closet), I got the 'all clear' to go play. Yes! Finally! BUT, I only had a short amount of time before dinner would be ready and I would need to be home. I rushed over to my friend's house and played as much as I could before the streetlights came on and I could hear my mom hollering for me to come home.

As a child, I never understood why I had to do certain things before I could do what I wanted to do. Even as an adult, this is still the case. I cannot meal prep if I do not clean the dishes. I cannot get dressed for the day if I do not take care of the laundry, and we all know laundry never ends. I cannot drive anywhere if I do not put gas in my car. I cannot go shopping if I do not have money, which means I have to go to work. The list goes on and on.

The First Step

Looking back on this moment, it is clear now that there were important biblical principles being instilled in me at a young age. God uses moments in our lives to build characteristics in us so we can be prepared for our future and what He plans to call us to. One of the hardest parts about walking in your calling is obedience. We don't think about how delay impacts our calling every time God calls us. I know I didn't at first.

We get so focused on the distractions of everyday life that we don't think about the consequences of neglecting our calling. Referring back to the story of Noah, could you imagine if he had delayed God's instructions? The flood would have come and the ark would not have been finished or, a much worse scenario, never started. The beautiful thing about God is His unfailing grace. Knowing that He directs our steps and though we stumble, we don't fall because

He's right there to offer us His sovereign hand (Psalm 37:23-24). However, this does not mean you have the ability to delay what you have been given.

Here's a real-life example. In 2019, I was a regular church attendee and served at Transformation Church in Tulsa, Oklahoma. At the beginning of every year, TC participates in a "21 Days of Prayer and Fasting," where the church focuses on fasting what they feel the Lord has asked them to give up for those 21 days. Each person will fast something different. This could be food, social media time, music, movies, and so on. Every day, you pray and fast, and each day has a theme for what to pray about.

This was my first time fasting and I decided to give up certain foods during my fasting journey, but I am not going to lie to you, I made it a solid 3 days before getting a drive thru chicken sandwich. And I have never loved the taste of chicken more in my life! Isn't it funny how fasting can do that to you? Anyways, that isn't the focus of this testimony. What happened during these 21 days of prayer is though. God was more focused on me giving Him my time in prayer then sacrificing protein options.

This season, I was applying for jobs and had just applied to work at a school in a very renowned district in Oklahoma. As a matter of fact, it was the top district in the area. During the second week of prayer and fasting, I started receiving a call from an unknown phone number during our church prayer session time. They would only call once and never leave a voicemail. This was strange as the church prayer session time was in the evening, so it was a little late for a job to be calling me, but it kept happening.

I thought it was a spam call or a bill collector, so I ignored it.

One night, they called after the prayer session had ended and I was able to answer. It was the school I applied for! They asked me to come in for an interview the following week. I was shocked to say the least. Now, I am sure you are expecting this story to have a happy ending. But sadly, due to my delayed obedience, it does not.

I was hired and started working for this school district. It was an exciting time! HR needed me to get them a couple documents to clear my background check and solidify employment. They gave me 30 days from my training start date to get this done. Every day in prayer, the Lord kept nudging me to get this done, but I just knew I had enough time. Not only did I wait until the last minute to get these documents in, but I remember the words that came from the woman in HR's voice over our phone call.

"Emily, I am so sorry, but at this time, due to the extreme delay in submitting these documents, we are no longer willing to accept them from you and, moving forward, we are retracting our offer to fully hire you. Thank you for your time in training, please turn in your badge and school property to our office."

God blessed me with the job I had prayed for, but my delay in finalizing the hiring process prevented me from moving forward in that job. This is not a story I have ever told, nor planned on telling, because of how ashamed I was for fumbling the blessing God gave me. However, God wanted me to use this example because it is going to set someone reading this on the right path of obedience. You can and will miss out on all God has for you if you do not remain obedient and steward well over what God blesses you with.

Now, did this experience hinder my career as an educator? Of course not. My calling has always been to work in education and that has been my career path for practically my entire life, glory to God. This was an opportunity to learn that God requires us to remain obedient when walking in our calling.

"And we know that God causes everything to work together for the good of those who love God and are called according to his purpose for them."
(Romans 8:28 NLT)

God has good plans for your life. It's up to you to follow His instructions and obey

His commands. How do you obey God?
With discipline and structure. Let's take a
look at how we these components impact
obedience.

DISCIPLINE

Remember when I said I was the
sassiest child? Well, my mother can
definitely attest to this. I can guarantee I got
in the most trouble as a kid and spent more
time in my room than any of my siblings (as
punishment and by choice). I wasn't a bad
child; just free spirited. Constantly getting
into things, very curious, and always talking,
even when I shouldn't have.

Now, I spent the most time with my
grandma in my adolescent years. At
grandma's house, she wanted me to be open
about everything. How I felt, what I liked

and disliked, even what I wanted to do when we were together. She embraced my extroverted bundle of crazy and taught me how to be the confident, adventurous woman I am today, living in freedom. Not letting anyone stomp on the bright light God put inside of me. May she rest in peace.

I quickly learned that grandma's house and mom's house were two different households. While my grandma wanted me to explore and embrace my wild side, my mom wanted a much different version of me. Her rules were stricter. She wanted to raise me to be a self-sufficient individual who could take care of myself. This wasn't something I could comprehend as an overly energized child seeking love and attention.

I didn't understand why I could eat what I wanted at grandmas, but I could not do that at moms. Or why I didn't have a bedtime routine at grandma's house, but when I stayed with my mom, it was teeth brushed and lights out by 8PM. I gave a lot of pushback and would find myself in trouble because of it. When I think about the difference in these two households, I think about how it has shaped my life as an adult. When transitioning from high school to college and finally living on my own, I went absolutely crazy! No bedtime, no routine, just doing whatever I wanted. Back to the ways of grandma's house. Sweet freedom!

When I say that it had the worst impact on my physical and mental health, I mean it. If you've never heard of the "Freshman 15," it's referring to the first year of college, where it is said that the average college freshman gains 15lbs that year. Well, I gained 20lbs in the first semester. It wasn't until my parents came to visit that my mom told me she was scared for my health because of how "bad I looked." She was worried about how much weight I had gained and how isolated I was, all spoken out of love.

I looked sick. And truthful, I was. Not having discipline created this version of myself that I struggled to love. Even today, I have had to work towards learning how to take care of and love myself the right way. The disciplined way. It's important to know how God feels about discipline.

"No discipline is enjoyable while it is happening – it's painful! But afterward there will be a peaceful harvest of right living for those who are trained in this way."
(Hebrews 12:11 NLT)

Discipline is often known as regulation. To have discipline is to have training or understanding of rules and commands. A word connected to discipline is direction. Discipline needs a direction. This means understanding what you must do in order to be successful in something. In other words, it's the work behind the assignment.

Obedience cannot be implemented without discipline. It takes discipline to actively do as God asks. When God gives you a calling, it is like an assignment. It is a task or a direction pointing you towards your purpose. Having discipline in your calling is staying on the path. It is doing the work your calling requires.

I like to think of discipline as the action of running. You can't finish a race if you stop running in the middle of it. If you are not staying disciplined, or putting in the work, you will not fulfill your calling. If you are not staying on the path, you will not be walking in the direction your life is supposed to go. Discipline keeps you moving towards everything God has for you.

The most important component of discipline is consistency. You hear this with people who work out on a regular basis. They will tell you their weight loss or muscle gain comes from the meal prep, workouts, water, and sleep they get every week. They have to walk in the direction of health and put in consistent work to see the results they are working towards. While consistency may be the most important component of discipline, one component that is not discussed enough is the sacrifice behind discipline.

Here's an example. To be completely transparent, God asked me to lose weight and make healthier choices years ago. I have struggled with this calling for a long time. I was finally diagnosed with PCOS after years of dieting and supplements. There are not enough words to describe the difficulty trying to maintain the symptoms that have come with this diagnosis. If you are someone or know someone who struggles with PCOS, you know exactly what I'm talking about. With that being said, God has continuously redirected my steps towards a healthier lifestyle.

This year, I made the decision that I would take control of my health once and for all. And guess what? That comes with sacrifice. There are things I cannot eat, events I cannot attend, and new priorities taking up space. Your calling will require you to sacrifice things you want for what God knows you need. That sacrifice will lead to the fulfillment of your calling.

God wants us to not just understand what discipline is, but to choose to live a life of discipline. Consistently waking up every day and choosing to actively work towards your calling, no matter what. Will it be easy? No. Will it be worth it? Yes. If this is an area you struggle in, you are not alone. Believe me, I am right there with you! And always remember that God is walking with you too. You are never alone. He loves you and wants you to succeed. This time next year, life will be different for all of us, because we now understand how important discipline is to our calling.

STRUCTURE

As much as my younger self contested cleaning her room, it was something that was absolutely necessary. This small task gave me an organized space that I could be proud of. It created an environment of cleanliness, comfort, and individuality. To this day, I carry the same pride when my home is clean and presentable to company. Maybe it's just me, but have you ever walked into your home and there was so much to clean you didn't know where to start? Or how about looking at a to-do list and seeing so many things that need to get done that it immediately overwhelms you? This is why structure is so important.

If you have never read the story of the Israelites being led by Moses to the wilderness, let me give you a playback. God revealed himself to Moses through a burning bush and told him to plead with pharaoh to let the Israelites go. Pharaoh's heart was hardened, so the Lord sent different plagues and catastrophes throughout Egypt until pharaoh finally allowed the Israelites to leave. There is so much more to that story, but the part we will focus on is the Israelites' time in the wilderness. I can name several sermons, books, even songs written about this story and its significance. But often times, what is missed are the specific detailed instructions the Israelites were given on how to worship, pray, serve, and live. If you don't believe me, read the book of Deuteronomy.

God had specific instructions for His people regarding how they were to be in the wilderness before they could enter into the "land flowing with milk and honey." He wanted them to sacrifice animals a specific way, build and enter the temple of worship in a certain way, remain clean through practices of purity specified by Him, and so much more. Why was all of this necessary? Why did God give them so many details and instructions to follow? Because structure is important to God.

For you to be successful in something, it has to have structure. Imagine running a race with no structure. How do you track who is running? What about the distance from start to finish? Is there a winner? Structure is necessary for your calling. What is structure? Organization. If you do not organize the calling God gives you, you will miss important details necessary for completing the calling. How can you obey commands that you have not organized and taken note of? You can't.

Let's go back to the story of Noah for just a second. God gave very specific instructions on how to build the ark. If Noah had missed even one detail, it could have been catastrophic to the structure of the ark, which could've majorly impacted its ability to sustain flotation and withstand the floodwaters. Often times, we get focused on the obedience of walking in our calling by staying disciplined in the things God has asked us to do, but we miss details because we haven't taken the time to organize the calling He gave us. Obedience cannot be fulfilled without structure.

It's kind of like going to the grocery store without a list. You know what you need, but it is easy to forget something when you didn't make a list of what you needed. You end up forgetting multiple things and grabbing stuff you didn't actually need, or even worse, getting everything except that one item that you really needed. Why? Because life can be distracting. Life can be complicated. Life can have messy situations. And if you're not careful, your lack of structure will cause a messy situation to become a messy life.

The Bible tells us to be sure that everything is done properly and in order (1 Corinthians 14:40 NLT). If you are walking in something you felt led by God to step into, but you feel stuck or stagnant, it may be that you need to go back to prayer and ask God if you missed an important detail when He instructed you before.

It could also mean that God is shifting you into a different position to continue walking in your calling, but in a new direction. This opens the door for God to be able to redirect you on the right path because you're not walking with Him at all like you thought you were. Though we will never know God's true intention because His ways and thoughts are nothing like ours, we can rest in knowing that He has plans to prosper us and give us a good future. With those plans come structure, so let's get organized together.

CHAPTER 3

TIME TO BREAKUP

When I first gave my life to God, it wasn't a full and total transformation. This was a process, and anyone who has given their life to God knows that the process of transformation can take some time. You don't become saved and go home living a perfect Christian life. That's not how this works. The day I gave my life to God, I went home to a toxic house and still had the same life and community I did before church that morning. Speaking of community, let's talk about a close friend I had during this time. For the sake of confidentiality, we will call her Jane.

I had known Jane for a couple years and she had been in my life through a lot of "unsaved" moments. From bars to boys and everything in between. Jane and I were together consistently. I admired Jane as she was very beautiful and a "popular girl" in my eyes. That was never me in any phase of life, even though I wanted to be. Once I gave my life to God, I really wanted to start living for Him, and there were things that I didn't desire to do anymore. I didn't want to have certain conversations. I didn't want to go to bars and talk to random boys. I wanted to go after God and actually have a relationship with Him. Jane couldn't understand this as she couldn't get past who I used to be.

I started identifying how one-sided our friendship really was. I did all of the driving when I would see her, I gave up so much time and committed to being there for her as much as I could. The hard truth I didn't want to face is that she wouldn't do the same for me and never did. The more I went after

God, the more toxic stuff started happening in our friendship. It got to a place where she started challenging my character as a "Christian" because of who I used to be, and how imperfect I still was, while making me question my value based on physical attributes and "unpopularity." I finally hit a point where I had to end this friendship. I knew it was *time to breakup.*

At the time our friendship was ending, I felt called by God to start setting things I used to do aside for things He wanted me to do more of. God wanted more of me. He wanted my time and attention. He wanted me to grow my knowledge of the Bible. There was no more time to be given to things from my past life because He wanted to make me into a new creation. I did not realize this would include giving up friendships.

Time to Breakup

Looking back, I didn't realize how much I compromised myself for someone who was never going to reciprocate the same love I gave them. I can't look back on a moment of our friendship and truly say that I enjoyed every conversation or every outing we went on together. There are moments where I will come across old pictures and videos and cringe because of who I used to be. Now, this is not to shame anyone! There are two sides to every story, this just happens to be mine.

What does any of this have to with your calling? Your calling from God will change the desires of your life. It will force you to "break up" with things of your past to have a better future with God. It sounds simple. But how these changes impact your life may not be.

PRUNING SEASON

When you are called by God, there are people, places, and things you will not be able to be around anymore. And if we are being honest, you won't want to be around them. It's important to know every change has a place in your calling. It might sting to let go of things you held love for, but this is how we transform. Let's call it your *pruning season.* If you've never walked through a season of pruning, you will. And when you do, it will feel exactly like a breakup – you will experience pain, growth, and new fruit.

To prune is to cut. The process of pruning is simply cutting away dead or overgrown things to increase growth and fruitfulness. When a tree has dead branches, they must be removed to make room for new branches. Have you ever seen a tree with dead branches bearing fruit? Neither have I.

What I have seen is a tree with healthy branches bearing fruit and dead branches impacting that fruit. If you refuse to remove what is dead or overgrown from your life, it can impact the fruit God is trying to produce in and through you. This is the part no one likes. Removing. Cutting away.

To us, we might see a friendship as fun and inviting, not realizing that God sees what we don't see and He knows this friendship is 'dead' or 'overgrown.' This goes for anything in your life. When something is cut or removed from us, it hurts. Cutting causes pain. This is why we try to hold on to people, places, and things as long as possible. Because even though we know it hurts us, even though we know this person is not good for us, even though we know living here is dangerous, even though we know this job is not where God wants us to stay, we hold tightly to what is familiar. We find comfort in familiarity.

There is a reason dead branches don't just fall off trees. God designed everything for a specific purpose. These branches were once healthy branches but have become dead or overgrown. They are a part of that tree but must be removed for its own good. This is a living example of why God has to prune us.

That person you love may have been good for you in the past, but they are no longer good for you, so God is trying to remove them to protect you. That house once provided you a safe home, but it's now a danger to you, which is why He is trying to move you to a different place. That job once provided you income that was sustainable for your life, but God wants to transition you to something better because the job no longer serves you. Pruning hurts

but is necessary for your growth. Once the
cutting has finished, this is where new
growth and fruit can be produced. Its only
after what is holding you back is removed
that you can start new growth.

LET GO AND LET GOD

Have you ever watched the Olympics?
One of the coolest sports to watch, in my
opinion, is gymnastics. The strength and
agility those athletes have is incredible. If
you are not familiar with gymnastics, the
sport is very rigid. Many strict rules are
implemented and must be followed for
safety. If an athlete breaks too many rules or
commits a series of violations, they can be
suspended or permanently ineligible to
compete, as with most sports. Don't believe
me? Look it up!

Why Me, God?

Do you know what I love about God, though? God does not hold anything we have done in the past against us. Isn't that cool? God loves us so much that He does not allow our past to disqualify us from the calling He has for our life and the blessings He wants to give us throughout. He doesn't keep record of all of our wrongdoings (1 Corinthians 13:4-5). Not even the world has the ability to disqualify us from what God has called us to (John 16:33).

We walk with God in the confidence that we are made new and that He has overcome this dark world we are temporarily living in. Now, what God will do is use your past. What you have been through in life is known as your testimony. There is power in your testimony. The things you have experienced help shape who you are and can help reach others for the kingdom of God.

Time to Breakup

There are many ways we can feel disqualified to move forward in our calling. No matter the sin. It could be drinking when you said you would finally go to AA or having sex before marriage when you said you would wait for your future spouse. Maybe it's gambling your hard-earned wages away or not spending time with God and trying to be your own savior. The list could go on forever. There will never come a time that you will feel qualified to step into your calling. That is the cold, hard truth. Nothing God calls you to will ever be comfortable. If you could do it comfortably, you wouldn't need God. This is the part where it's time to break up… with shame.

If God doesn't keep past records, why are you? The Bible tells us there is no condemnation with Christ (Romans 8:1). In order to fully walk in our calling, we must let go and let God. There is nothing that can disqualify you from what God has for you, except you. If you choose not to accept the calling, that's on you. If you choose to walk in shame, that is also on you. At the end of the day, we know that we don't have to live in shame, for we have been made new through Christ Jesus. (2 Corinthians 5:17). Letting go of shame is easier said than done.

If you let God in, He can help heal the shame you feel. God wants us to give everything we are worried about, everything we are anxious of, and every doubt or fear we have to Him. God cares about you (1 Peter 5:7). Don't disqualify yourself when God has called and qualified you. If the creator of the universe believes you can do it, you should trust Him. He has a track record of victory.

CHAPTER 4

A NEW CREATION

Have you ever played the game *Sims*? It was one of my favorites growing up! I always loved designing people with their own style, personality, career, and all the other fun things they got to do. Sometimes, I would move them to different houses, change their jobs, and build up different skills, essentially making them into a new person. Funny enough, when you give your life to God, that's exactly what He does with you. Your life is no longer your own. You are a new creation in Christ and He is directing your steps.

He will ask you to move places, change careers, give up friendships for new ones, change churches, serve in different areas, and do things you wouldn't do without His guidance and instruction. The steps He directs you to take are all connected to the calling He has given you. If you have been walking with God for some time, you know exactly what I mean. If you are new to walking with God, how exciting! Welcome… and buckle up!

Being a new creation in Christ refers to laying down your old life for your new life with God. What does that mean? It means accepting and believing in the salvation we receive through Jesus Christ. The calling God has on your life is directly connected to your salvation. In order for God to call you, you must be saved. God cannot call someone who has not fully accepted God for who He is, and what He has done to give us redeeming grace.

"For this is how God loved the world: He gave his one and only Son, so that

everyone who believes in him will not perish
but have eternal life."
(John 3:16 NLT)

The calling God places on your life is directly connected to the people He wants you to impact for the kingdom of God. It's to save souls. How can God use you to save others if you are not fully saved yourself? It's like asking someone to teach you how to drive a car when they have never actually learned how to drive a car themselves. That wouldn't make very much sense now would it? No, it would not. So, what does being saved look like? Let's talk about it.

LET'S TALK ABOUT JESUS

The Bible tells us two important steps to take when becoming a new creation in

Christ. The first step you must take is accepting Jesus into your heart and confessing with your mouth that He is Lord. This is your acknowledgment of what God has done as the ultimate sacrifice. Romans 10:9 NLT tells us, "If you openly declare that Jesus is Lord and believe in your heart that God raised him from the dead, you will be saved." Acknowledging and accepting the death and resurrection of Jesus Christ in your heart is what gives you salvation. If you don't know, salvation is the deliverance of sin. When you accept Jesus Christ as your Lord and Savior, you are delivered from sin.

When looking at the life of Jesus, he demonstrated how we should live. Jesus was baptized by John the Baptist and lived a life of purity and honesty. He preached the word of God and helped people understand God's true love and the nature of repentance. He walked in his calling and stayed obedient to

God throughout his life, and even when he struggled, he still chose God's will over his own. Jesus died on the cross, taking all of our sin and shame from us, to give us new life with God. What a beautiful sacrifice we did not deserve!

This leads us to the second step we must take when becoming saved: getting baptized. Before Jesus began his ministry, or stepped into his calling, he was baptized. God wants us to experience baptism because of what it signifies. Baptism represents washing away your sins and being made new. It is a physical representation of laying down your old life for your new life.

When you are being dipped in the water, you are allowing your old life to wash away, and as you arise, you are made a new creation. It is a symbolization of purification. How can you be a new creation in Christ if you do not leave your old life behind? You can't. This is a necessary step.

If you are a new Christian, or maybe you've been walking with God for a while and just haven't taken this step yet, baptism might be a touchy subject for you. Maybe you're scared because you feel like your life has to look a certain way before you can get baptized. Maybe you don't feel worthy of baptism because there are things you refuse to give up and you don't believe you will really be "clean." Maybe you feel guilty because you've waited so long to get baptized and now it just seems irrelevant. Whatever your reasoning may be, know that God is with you through every step.

God doesn't expect you to come to Him already perfect. He doesn't expect you to be dunked in the water and automatically have a changed life. God wants to walk with you in your imperfection. He wants to help you change day by day and He wants to take the guilt, shame, and pain away from you. That's why He sent Jesus to the cross. That's why we have salvation.

Baptism allows us to wash all of that away and, even though we are still imperfect people, we get to live a life with a beautiful God who forgets our past sins. We will never be able to do anything that will be worthy enough or pure enough. It's why we need Jesus. Refusing baptism because you want to 'clean up first' is like saying Jesus' blood isn't enough. Remember, being saved has two steps. Your calling depends on both.

THE TRUE LIVING WORD

This section is short but more than necessary. As much as I love sharing parts of my life with you and embracing the power of my testimony through this book, the most important book you will ever need is the Bible. The Bible is the true, living word of God, and it is the closest we will get to God on this earth other than through His spirit. If you have not spent a lot of time in the Bible, I encourage you to start. Even if it's one chapter a day, the more you spend time in God's word, the more God can reveal himself to you.

Every story in the Bible helps connect you to God and His character. It gives lineage, historic timelines, instructions on how to live your life, and what expectations God has for you as a new creation in Christ. The book of Revelation teaches us what is to come, though I recommend starting with Genesis or Matthew before trying to expert level deep dive into the word of God. Let's walk before we run.

A New Creation

Learning the word of God helps you to understand how to live your life as a new creation. Find a translation that helps you understand what you are reading and connect with God in a new way or find a devotional that you can follow. My preferred translation in the New Living Translation. If you struggle to comprehend what you are reading, get connected to community who can help shed light on your confusion. Make reading the Bible a priority. I promise you it is worth it.

CHAPTER 5

CALLING VS. PURPOSE

One of the most uncomfortable feelings
you can have as a child is starting school in
a new place. When I was growing up, my
mom moved us often as she would change
jobs for better pay. She followed the money,
but she had to in order to take care of my
siblings and me. We moved a lot. For
reference, from the age of 10 to 15 years
old, we moved 6 times. All different cities
across different states. As you can imagine,
this made it difficult to make friends.

As I stated before, I was never a
"popular" girl. I've always had a hard time
making friends because I was heavily
bullied in elementary school. This made me
skeptical of making any friends as it created
insecurity in me at a young age. The first

day at a new school is always the hardest. All of your classmates stare at you because you are the new kid they don't know. Everyone has their cliques and are not looking to expand, so you just awkwardly move around your day trying to seem as normal as possible so people will talk to you.

You don't want to be too loud or answer too many questions during lessons, just keep your head down and be what I have come to identify as a "reserved friendly." The absolute worst part of the day is lunch. Figuring out where to sit and hoping people don't think you eat in a weird way or judging how much you eat. It feels like a nightmare. One I had to relive often.

As school would end on that dreadful first day, I would rush to the bus or race home as fast as I could to hide in my room. I just wanted to be in my safe space. My family never understood this and it wasn't something I could explain to them because none of them looked like me. All of my siblings looked the same. Blonde hair, light colored eyes, skinny, beautiful. I'm a bigger girl with dark colored hair and dark colored eyes. The more we moved, the more I judged my appearance and wished I looked like my family because, maybe then, I would have friends. I felt so alone.

I knew of God when I was a child, but I did not actually *know* Him. I remember sitting in my room and always asking God the same question:

"Why me, God?"

This question went through my head in every situation I encountered throughout my life. I found myself asking this question more and more every day:

"Why ME, God?"

Then more questions would proceed:

"Why do people hate the way I look so
much?"
"Why can't I make any friends?"
"Why can't I look like the rest of my
family?"
"Why does life have to be this way?"

The list of questions could stretch a
mile long. It was only recently that God
gave me the answer to this never-ending
question. The main question I had asked
Him for so much of my life. If you've ever
had this question arise in your mind, let me
give you the answer:

**It's all part of your calling, which is
connected to your purpose.**

Such a simple sentence with such a complex meaning. My purpose... what exactly is my purpose? What does that even mean? Isn't this book about God's calling on your life? What does my calling have to do with my purpose? I know you want answers, so let's dive in.

YOU WERE MADE FOR THIS

A common question we find ourselves asking in everyday life is "What is the purpose of this?" Whether it's an email from work asking to schedule a meeting, or maybe it's a movie with a weird plot. I've even asked this question in rush hour traffic watching cars practically wreck into each other trying to merge. The same goes for our very existence. Have you ever wondered why you were here? Have you ever wondered what purpose God had in creating you? I know I have. Before we can understand God's purpose for our lives, we must understand what the meaning of purpose is.

The purpose of something is the reason for which something was created. Another way of saying this is the reason why something exists. To understand your God given purpose in this world, you first need to understand how God created you. Here are a few scriptures in the Bible that talk about God creating us:

"Then God said, "Let us make human beings in our image, to be like us. They will reign over the fish in the sea, the birds in the sky, the livestock, all the wild animals on the earth, and the small animals that scurry along the ground."
(Genesis 1:26 NLT)

*"You made all the delicate, inner parts
of my body and knit me together in my
mother's womb. Thank you for making me
so wonderfully complex! Your workmanship
is marvelous—how well I know it. You
watched me as I was being formed in utter
seclusion, as I was woven together in the
dark of the womb. You saw me before I was
born. Every day of my life was recorded in
your book. Every moment was laid out
before a single day had passed."*
(Psalms 139:13 -16 NLT)

*"... for through him God created
everything in the heavenly realms and on
earth. He made the things we can see and
the things we can't see— such as thrones,
kingdoms, rulers, and authorities in the
unseen world. Everything was created
through him and for him."*

Calling vs. Purpose

(Colossians 1:16 NLT)

God designed us in His image. He created us to be like Him and with Him always. His plan started in the garden of Eden. God's intention for creating us was and always has been to be with us and take care of us. To love us. Think about humans for a second. Why do we have children? Why do we have a desire to reproduce? I'll answer that question with scripture:

> *"Take delight in the Lord, and he will give you your heart's desires."*
> *(Psalms 37:4 NLT)*

When you have a relationship with God and submit to His plan, He plants desires in your heart. Your maternal or paternal instinct is directly related to God and how

He made you. God is our Father. Your desire to be a parent reflects His image. It's the reason why parents will go to the end of the earth for their children. It is God's design. It is what He did and does for us. This is just one example of a desire God gives us. Now, I understand this can bring other questions, such as:

"If that's the case, how come there are couples that cannot have children, even though they have a desire to be parents?"

"Why do some people that don't desire to have child have them?"

"How come unplanned pregnancies happen and there are children growing up without parents all over the world?"

All of these questions are valid. And I know there are so many more that could be asked inside of this specific topic. I have found myself asking these same questions at times. There is one Bible verse that I can give you to reference.

"My thoughts are nothing like your thoughts," says the Lord. "And my ways are far beyond anything you could imagine."
(Isaiah 55:8 NLT)

I will never be able to explain to you why God does what He does. Nobody will. Because none of us will ever be able to fully comprehend who He truly is and how He thinks. There are forces beyond what we can see. God is the creator of all things, in heaven and on earth. Each one of us is designed uniquely, but all in His image. Each one of us has lived different lives from one another, and yet we have experienced His love, grace, and spiritual intervention.

I am certain every person in this world has experienced a miracle they cannot explain. From a random check in the mail coming at just the right time to sickness or disease miraculously healing when doctors pronounced it incurable. Our takeaway: God moves in mysterious ways. By choosing to believe in God and the salvation He gave us through Jesus Christ, you choose to accept that there are questions you may never receive answers to. But one thing we do know is that our God is love. And He does all things in love. Including creating us.

"We know how much God loves us, and we have put our trust in his love. God is love, and all who live in love live in God, and God lives in them."

(1 John 4:16 NLT)

God created you because He loves you. He saw the plans He had for you long before you were created and His intention for creating you was to use you and the desires He gives you. This is where we dive into purpose. God created each and every one of us with a distinct purpose. Your purpose is different from your calling. Purpose is why we exist. Here are some scriptures that refer to our God given purpose:

"That's the whole story. Here now is my final conclusion: Fear God and obey his commands, for this is everyone's duty."
(Ecclesiastes 12:13 NLT)
"Jesus came and told his disciples, "I have been given all authority in heaven and on earth. Therefore, go and make disciples of all the nations, baptizing them in the name of the Father and the Son and the Holy Spirit. Teach these new disciples to obey all the commands I have given you.

Why Me, God?

And be sure of this: I am with you always,
even to the end of the age."
(Matthew 28:18-20 NLT)

"So, whether you eat or drink, or
whatever you do, do it all for the glory of
God."
(1 Corinthians 10:31 NLT)

"And this world is fading away, along
with everything that people crave. But
anyone who does what pleases God will live
forever."
(1 John 2:17 NLT)

Our purpose in this world is to represent
God to others. We live in a fallen world.
From the moment the fruit was consumed in
the garden of Eden, we had separation from
God. We had sin. The consequence of sin
was our banishment from the place God
created for us to dwell with Him forever.

However. It is not in God's nature as a loving Father to leave us in this world alone.

Remember, God IS love. He created us to do life with Him. This is why God sent Jesus to die on the cross. To give us salvation. To give us a way back to Him. Because Jesus took the cross, we now have undeserved privilege and believing in his death and resurrection gives us everlasting life. This world is temporary. Our life with God is eternal. Your purpose from God is to live your life as Christ lived.

"You must have the same attitude that Christ Jesus had. Though he was God, he did not think of equality with God as something to cling to. Instead, he gave up his divine privileges; he took the humble position of a slave and was born as a human being. When he appeared in human form, he humbled himself in obedience to God and

died a criminal's death on a cross."
(Philippians 2:5-8 NLT)

To walk in purpose is to understand that we must live in love. God created us to serve and love, and our example of this is given through the life Jesus. The more we walk in purpose, the more we reflect God's character and His image that dwells within us. How do we live this way? By allowing God to direct our steps. This is the value of your calling. Your calling is connected to your purpose.

The calling God has placed on your life is significant to you and you alone. We have all been created with the purpose of living our lives for God and having faith to trust Him. We have all been designed to love others as Christ loved the church. Your calling is not your purpose, but they are directly connected.

YOU WERE DESIGNED FOR THIS

Every person I have ever met in this world has heard this question asked at least once in their life:

"What do you want to be when you grow up?"

Usually, it's at a kindergarten graduation, where the school district will trust a five-year-old with a microphone. Some of those answers are common occupations, while others are out-of-pocket responses that bring laughter to millions through viral videos. There's a reason why the show *Kids Say the Darndest Things* was so popular in the 90s, before social media. But when was the last time someone asked this question to an adult? Has someone ever looked at you at the ripe age of 26 and

asked, "What you wanted to BE?"
Generally, the question changes, and we
often hear "What do you want to DO with
your life?"

Being the sassy child I was, every time
someone would ask me what I wanted to be
when I grew up, I would tell them "A
superstar, duh!" I just knew I would be
famous like Britney Spears or Christina
Aguilera. Traveling and touring all over the
world, singing songs and dancing on stages
everywhere. Obviously, that is not my life
story. But your girl had dreams. She still
does! Those dreams have just evolved.
Being a pop star is definitely not my dream
now, but music has always been a staple in
my life. When I had nothing, I had music.
I've always had God, and I know the desire
to create music and work in the field of
music was planted in my heart by Him.

Today, my career revolves around
teaching music to people of all age ranges. If
you had asked me years ago if I would be a
music teacher, the answer would've been no.
But God had other plans, and I'm so grateful
He did. I wouldn't do anything else with this
life than be a music teacher. And isn't it so
funny that I dreaded new schools as a child,
but now pray to have the ability to teach
everywhere? God really does have a sense
of humor.

I shared this part of my testimony with
you for this reason: each one of us is
designed uniquely. We have all been blessed
with different gifts and desires. You're
calling is directly connected to the gifts God
has blessed you with. There are a multitude
of spiritual gifts referenced in the Bible,
including, but not limited to: administration,
prophecy, teaching, hospitality, and even
evangelism (1 Corinthians 12:7-10).

Spiritual gifts are designated by God as He decides which gifts each person shall receive (1 Corinthians 12:11). The most important thing to understand about spiritual gifts is the reason behind them.

"There are different kinds of spiritual gifts, but the same Spirit is the source of them all. There are different kinds of service, but we serve the same Lord. God works in different ways, but it is the same God who does the work in all of us."

(1 Corinthians 12:4-6 NLT)

Your spiritual gifts are given to you for your calling. The assignment God gives you will be tied directly to the spiritual gifts He designates to you. While we all have the ability to inhabit different spiritual gifts listed in the Bible at different periods of our lives, our gifts come to us specifically from God.

"Are we all apostles? Are we all prophets? Are we all teachers? Do we all have the power to do miracles? Do we all have the gift of healing? Do we all have the ability to speak in unknown languages? Do we all have the ability to interpret unknown languages? Of course not!"
(1 Corinthians 12:29-30 NLT)

And I can already hear your question…

"Why are we talking about spiritual gifts and what does this have to do with your calling?"

We must understand that, though our spiritual gifts are different, they are designed for one purpose, and that is to be the body of Christ (1 Corinthians 12:27). Remember, your purpose is to live your life for God as an example to the world. Your calling is connected to your purpose. Our purpose connects us as one body for God designed us to love and serve one another. To be disciples and be a light to the dark world we live in.

We have a good understanding of our purpose, now we need to understand calling. A calling is a strong urge towards a particular way of life. Another definition is a pull toward something you feel drawn to or passionate about. Your calling is an assignment designated by God. This can be anything from your career to your future spouse. God calls us to people, places, and things designated for us.

You can have more than one calling on your life. While you may feel called to work in finance, you may also feel called to work with and serve teenagers through youth ministry. It is possible to have multiple callings from God. Where God calls you is

up to Him, but the way to know what you
are called to is through direct connection to
God. Let's go back to the beginning of this
chapter. Do you remember the part where
we discussed the desires of your heart? Here
is the scripture:

*"Take delight in the Lord, and he will
give you your heart's desires."*
(Psalms 37:4 NLT)

The desires planted in your heart by
God are used for your calling. As you walk
with the Lord, He will lead and guide you
through your calling. God directs us towards
different careers, friend groups, and even
churches. Your calling is specific to you. It
is why you were born into that family. It's
why you have always felt a tug towards that
career path. It's why you just knew you
were to serve in that area of ministry. As

you trust in the Lord and allow Him to guide your steps, He will give you a desire for your calling and equip you with the gifts to fulfill it.

"And we know that God causes everything to work together for the good of those who love God and are called according to his purpose for them."
(Romans 8:28 NLT)

Every time you ask the question "Why me, God?" I want you to remember this:

You were designed for this.

God knew the world needed you. God knew your calling would put you in the path of people who need to see God through you. You are a light. You are made in His image. Your calling allows you to be connected to people that He wants you to impact for the kingdom of God. You were once lost, but now you are found. And your life is now a dedication to God and helping others know Him so they, too, can share in eternal life with God. Everything you go through in life is connected to your calling. It's your testimony.

Your testimony will influence people who have experienced similar life events or feelings of loneliness, insecurity, and pain. Your testimony has power. And your calling will help you reach people others cannot reach because God designed for you to reach them. It was His plan all along. So, the next time you question why you're here, just remember that God uniquely created you. He has a purpose for your life. He's called you. He's always with you. And most importantly, He loves you.

CHAPTER 6

IT'S NOT ABOUT YOU

Teachers do not get paid enough. There, I said it. No one could've prepared me for a career as an educator for many reasons. The hardest part about being a teacher is trying to survive on what feels like little to no income. Do not get me wrong, I have been blessed beyond measure, and I thank God for every opportunity and paycheck He has allowed me to receive because Lord knows it could always be worse. I will say… it is hard in these streets. Many people do not know the expectations placed on teachers.

You know those nicely decorated classrooms your students have? Most teachers pay out-of-pocket to make that happen. Things like fidget toys, extra snacks, sanitation and hygiene products, even additional safety mechanisms to protect our students from outside threats are all things most teachers pay for with their own hard-earned money. It is prioritized as a requirement and a necessity to ensure students are able to have the learning environment they need, but somehow, this falls to the individual responsibility of the teacher. If you have a student in school or a loved one who is an educator, thank those teachers and pray for them. Ask them if there's anything they need. Lord knows it would mean the world to them.

As a music teacher, I have found myself working other jobs or side hustles during breaks and summertime. This second income provides cushion to make sure my classroom has everything that it needs and that I am able to pay my bills and feed myself. My side hustle of choice is being a rideshare driver. I started doing this because

Why Me, God?

it offered me the ability to make extra
money on my own time. Is it the safest job?
No. I thank God every day that I have had
kind passengers that haven't tried to hurt
me. And yes, I could tell you some crazy
stories! There is one I will share as it
pertains to calling.

One night, I received a ride request to
pick someone up from the airport and drive
them almost an hour across town. That's far!
I was about to decline it, but the Lord
nudged my heart to accept and complete this
ride. I had no idea why, and honestly, I was
annoyed. It was towards the end of my
"shift" and I was already close to home, so
this was out of the way. But I obeyed. In my
mind, I was thinking I would have to help
load tons of luggage into my car and risk
potentially hauling a group of loud, chaotic
passengers across the city. The closer I got
to the airport, the more frustrated I was.

"God, I don't want to do this one."

No response from God. Cool. As I got to the airport, there was a woman standing alone with just one bag. She did not need my help and she got in the car quickly. I tried speaking with her at first, but she didn't really talk to me. I could tell there was a sadness, but I wanted to give her space. After all, I really didn't even want to drive her. After a few minutes of driving, she started opening up the conversation. I couldn't tell you at the time what caused the floodgates to open, but she began pouring out her current circumstances to me. I can tell you now that this was definitely God.

This woman sobbed in my backseat, explaining how she had just lost her mother and describing all the hardship she was feeling as she prepared to bury her mom.

She was only home for a short amount of time before she would have to go back for her mother's funeral. For the remainder of this 50-minute ride, we shared stories of our families and, somehow, the conversation led to God. We were able to discuss how incredible the Lord is and how, even in our sorrow and pain, He is our comforter and brings peace.

I had never prayed over someone in my car before, but I felt the Lord nudge me to pray with her. I asked her if she would allow me to pray for her and she was more than excited about it! We held hands, wept together, and prayed to the Lord. As I finished the prayer, she looked directly into my eyes and said "God knew I needed you. Thank you. I will never forget this moment for the rest of my life." She got into my car broken and she left my car with peace. Once she exited the car, God said something to me I never considered until that moment.

"It was never about you."

Your calling isn't about you. When God calls you to something, He calls you with intentionality. You are the vessel He uses because He knows you are who others need in that moment in time. Of all the people in this world, also created by God, He called you. That sounds scarier than it really is. The reason it sounds scary is because it is heavy. The weight of being a vessel can feel overwhelming in situations you feel underprepared for. I have news for you: you will never feel prepared to be used by God.

We are not worthy of God and His unfailing love. We are reminded of that every time we walk towards God. Why do you think you have so much shame? Do you think you are the only person that feels that way? Why is it that every time God asks us to do something, we immediately think of reasons why we can't or shouldn't do it? It would be much easier to live life the way we want to. Or so we think. This is how people have lived for years, which is why our world is so dark. Conforming to the world fills you with darkness because this world is a dark place. But God calls us to be different. He calls us to be light.

Have you ever had the power go out in your home? What is the first thing you do? Usually when this happens, you try and locate a flashlight or candle. Why? Because you need to see. You need light. That is what you are. As a new creation in Christ, you are a light to the world. And as you walk with God, He lights the path you are to take. Remember, your calling is a strong urge towards something. As you get closer to God, He will give you a strong urge towards people, places, and things you would've never otherwise been connected to or around. And as you walk with God, it becomes easier to let go of shame and be used by Him.

THAT'S OFF LIMITS

Your calling has limits. This might sound strange as our God is limitless and outside of time and space. However, you are not God. You can only do so much as one person. God knows this, which is why He gave us specific instructions written in the Bible on how to live our lives. Our God loves us so much that He knew we needed parameters. Our calling falls within those parameters.

If you've ever driven a car at night, you know exactly what I'm talking about. Each lane of a highway only has so much space. In order to merge, you must use your signal to show others you are transitioning to a new lane. You can't operate a car at night without your lights on, otherwise, you wouldn't be able to see the parameters of the lane or the signage directing you where you are going. Get to the point, Emily. Got it, here we go.

Your purpose is the highway. Your calling is the lane you are driving in. To protect yourself and others, there are parameters around your calling that limit you to specific people, places, and things. Sometimes, God will change your life completely, taking you in a new direction and on a new path. Remember, your calling is designated by God, so He directs your steps and will transition you as needed. This

It's Not About You

is all part of your purpose, just shifting lanes. Your car is your life with God. It is what helps you be a light to the world. Just as you upgrade vehicles and lighting mechanisms change, so does your light. The more you evolve with God and spend time with Him, the brighter your light becomes.

Thinking of your calling in this way, you must understand limits are for your safety. If we didn't have lines to show us the separation between lanes, we would have way more car accidents than we already do. God does not want you to stray from your lane. You are to walk in your calling and be obedient to your limits. Why is this necessary? To protect yourself and others. These limits are called boundaries.

Your calling is only meant to reach specific people. If you do not have boundaries, you will welcome anyone in. This is dangerous for you as evil comes to snuff out light. The brighter your light is, the more people you will attract. And while we are called to reach the lost, we are not called to every person. This is why we need discernment.

As a new creation in Christ, we are led by God through discernment. Discernment is the ability to judge a situation based on spiritual guidance. We lean on God to help guide us and give us the ability to judge a situation in the right context. This is for our protection. You ever had a gut feeling about someone or felt like you needed to get away from the place you were currently at? That's called intuition.

Derived from discernment, intuition is the ability to understand something immediately. It is instinctual. An unexplainable feeling to move. The Lord will help guide you towards and away from different things in order to protect you and keep you in your lane. If you're in your lane, you will not encounter anyone or anything you shouldn't.

THE CHOICE IS YOURS

Though our calling is designated by God, we still have free will to choose whether or not we will fulfill that calling. The concept of free will is hard for many people to understand. We like to justify the things that happened in our lives by saying things like:

"Whatever is supposed to happen will happen."
"If it's meant to be, it will be."
"God will work everything out."

These statements are absolutely true…
if you are following the Lord's instructions
for your life. These statements are
absolutely not true if you are walking your
own path. For example, if someone comes
into your life and you bond with them, but
they are encouraging you to compromise
things you know the Lord has asked you to
stand firm on, such as purity or discipline,
you now have a choice. You can choose to
disconnect from this person and allow
yourself to stand firm with God or you can
choose to compromise for this person. This
is free will. And yes, it is true that God
knows what is going to happen before it
happens.

*So why doesn't God stop us from
choosing outside of His ways?*

Because if He did, it wouldn't be love. God is love. God created us because He loves us. Just like you want to be chosen by those you love, God wants to be chosen by you. He wants you to love Him enough to choose His calling for your life. If we didn't have free will, it wouldn't be love, it would be dictatorship. This is why we have the freedom to choose the life that we want to live. You can choose to live for God and lay down your wants for God's calling on your life. You can also choose to walk your own path. Every decision matters. The decision you make will either be met with reward or consequence.

God blesses those who trust in Him and follow His plan for their life. When we choose outside of God, we choose to take on the consequence of our actions. If you choose to stay connected to someone who is asking you to compromise your morals, you are actively choosing to allow distance in your relationship with God. The closer you are drawn to this individual, the further they will take you from Him. This experience can create further damage in your life and hinder you from fulfilling your calling or being connected to God altogether.

Experiences also have the ability to create generational bondage, which is something you will pass onto your children if not healed. God will never send someone into your life that will ask you to live outside of His boundaries for you. He will never direct you to encounter a person that will take His place on the throne of your heart. This is just one example of how a choice can impact your relationship with God and the calling He has for your life. You must stand firm on your decision to trust God and His plans.

Your calling is not about you. Your calling uses you for others who need salvation. This doesn't mean your calling is for everyone. If you take anything away from this chapter, I pray you ask God to show you if the people you are connected to are who He truly wants you to be connected to.

I pray you have the strength to allow God to transition you into the lane you belong in so that you are able to impact the right people. If there is anyone that is not supposed to be around you, I pray that God would reveal this to you, and you would have the strength to choose God over your own wants. Our plans might seem great, but God's plans will always be greater.

CHAPTER 7

HOSTAGE NEGOTIATION

"Come out with your hands up."

We all know the nail-biting scene where the criminals have taken hostages and law-enforcement is trying to negotiate for their safety.

"If you come out with your hands up, we won't have to use force against you."

You sit on the edge of your seat, waiting to see what happens. Will the criminals let the hostages go? Will they find a way to escape the law? How long will the police wait before they storm the building and use necessary force to save lives? How long is this going to take? When will this end?!

Personally, my movie genre of choice is comedy. I enjoy a good laugh with a wholesome plot. Action movies are a close second though. There's something about the cinematic drama that really gets my blood pumping. Watching and waiting for the scene where the good guys conquer the bad guys. These scenes are usually where the plot of the movie unfolds and things start moving.

Hostage negotiations, however, are not my favorite. Every scene that shows hostages has a similar feel. The bad guys are trying to figure out a way to escape without being caught or losing their lives. The hostages are afraid and trying to devise a plan to escape the criminals. Law-enforcement is getting set up and trying to communicate with the criminals for possible release of the hostages and surrender. Same scene, different movie.

Have you ever looked at your life as a hostage negotiation? That's a weird question to ask someone. It does have merit though. I don't know about you, but I am constantly having to reevaluate my feelings, past experiences, and trauma. There are moments in my walk with God where He has asked me to do something and I struggled to follow through because of bondage.

What do you mean by bondage?

Bondage is the feeling of being bound or tied to something. Bondage keeps us from experiencing the fullness of freedom with God. Often times, bondage looks like a past experience we encountered and never healed from or trauma we repressed. When you walk with God and carry bondage, you will experience moments of hesitation or delay in your obedience to do what God has asked you to do. For me, it feels like my spirit is being held captive by what I've encountered and God is trying to negotiate for my freedom.

Do you know what the worst part about a hostage negotiation is? How long it can take to be resolved. When you live in bondage, it can hinder your ability to walk with God for long periods of your life. Bondage can develop feelings of fear or anxiety, which can hinder your ability to move in the way that you need to. It can paralyze you. Bondage, if you are not careful, can alter the course of your life and impact generations after you. This is known as generational bondage.

Have you ever noticed that you experience things in your life similar to the experiences your parents or grandparents had? Things like struggles with money, toxic relationships, or instability in work and home life? That is what generational bondage is. Bondage that was not conquered or dealt with by someone in your family line before you, so it was passed down generations until it reached you. We carry bondage for things we have experienced, but we also carry generational bondage for things our family generations before us experienced. Welcome to the world of spiritual warfare.

The hardest thing you will ever do is conquer your bondage. Spiritual warfare is exactly what it sounds like. War in the spiritual realm. Bondage is ties attached to our spirit that prevent us from moving forward in certain situations because of our captivity to what is keeping us bound. The Bible tells us we do not fight in flesh, but we fight in spirit. The Bible also tells us that fear is not from God. There is a war being waged for your soul every day. The more you walk with God, the harder life gets. Do you know why? Because we live in sinful nature. But there is something else you should know: there is an enemy after your soul.

We have an "enemy?"

We sure do. Should you be afraid? Absolutely not! God has already won the victory. God will give you the ability to crush Satan under your feet. He holds you with his victorious hand and helps you walk through the darkest valleys. God is with you in everything, including your fight to conquer your bondage. The more you walk with God, the more apparent your bondage will become. This is your opportunity for freedom. This is your moment to escape. To stop being a hostage.

IT WAS A SETUP

In any good action movie, there is always a "plot twist." Something happens that you didn't see coming. The good guy is actually the bad guy. There was more to the plot than initially revealed. A surprise new character makes an appearance. It was a setup! Something that adds dramatic effect to an already intense situation.

When the "plot twist" occurs, the outcome is still the same, it just means there was more to conquer or deal with than initially planned. How interesting. Have you ever encountered a "plot twist" moment in your life? I know I have! Especially as I have walked through my calling.

As you walk with God and embrace your calling, you will encounter "plot twist" moments. These are moments where something happens that you could not have prepared for. When we encounter a "plot twist," it doesn't change the outcome. When God makes a promise, He fulfill His promise. When God says something is going to happen, it is going to happen. Therefore, when a "plot twist" occurs, we know it's a setup.

A setup? What does that mean?

A setup is the way something is organized or arranged. The setup was always part of the plan. Everything you go through is a setup for your breakthrough. God is the author and finisher. He knows the path He's leading you down. He designed it. He knows exactly what you will encounter.

He factored in every "plot twist" moment you would experience. He sets us up. Now, why would God do that? For your breakthrough.

Experiencing a setup can sometimes feel like a setback. A setback is the opposite of breakthrough. A setback is reversing progress. A breakthrough is an important discovery that aids in progress. When we experience a setup, we discover something important that we did not know before it occurred. The reason this can sometimes feel like a setback is due to the fact that it reveals something we didn't initially know, which feels like we are starting over or backing up. This is not the case. God incorporates setups in our lives to reveal important discoveries about circumstances, situations, and obstacles we go through in order to succeed. The outcome is still the same, we just have more to deal with.

Why would God do this?

To help you grow. If you never have a breakthrough in your life, you will never experience important discoveries about the things you have gone through or are currently going through. Without these important discoveries, you will lack key insights that will not only help you reach the outcome God has for you, but you will repeat circumstances, or cycles, that will keep you from making progress.

Cycles are repeated sets of events. What is a setback again? Reversing progress. Cycles will take us in reverse when we should be moving forward. They are literal setbacks. When you are walking down a path and have to back up for any reason, you will have to encounter that part of the path you've already walked on again. Why? The

path doesn't change because you backed up.
It's still the same path.

This is why we feel like we go through
situations that have mimicked other
moments in our lives. When you encounter
similar situations, there is a reason. God is
trying to set you up for breakthrough. He
wants you to discover something important
that will help you move forward down the
path He has paved for you and not get stuck
in reverse. We need to experience the setup
so we can experience the breakthrough. This
is how we will conquer cycles to fulfill all
God has called us to.

THE ULTIMATE MANIPULATOR

In high school, I was actively involved
in church. From leading worship in youth
and adult services to helping with outreach

and kids' ministry. I spent the majority of
my teenage years in church. All that time in
the church and I was never taught about who
Satan actually is. It still blows my mind
today. The only time the church referenced
Satan is when they talked about him being
"the enemy that has already been defeated."
Don't get me wrong, that is 100% true, but
there is so much more that we need to
know.

*Who is Satan and where did he come
from?*

Satan is known as "the devil," which
means the "enemy of God." Satan is actually
Lucifer, an angel created by God. He was a
guardian surrounding the throne of God.
Lucifer became filled with pride and wanted
a throne above God, so he was cast down to
earth alongside other angels he had

corrupted. Now, he roams the earth. His mission is to steal, kill, and destroy lives.

Why is he our "enemy?"

His name means "enemy of God." We were created by God for God. We were created to love God and be loved by God. We are made in the image of God. Everything about us revolves around God. Our existence is an acknowledgment of God's authority and power. When we walk in our calling, we surrender ourselves to God's will for our lives.

Our calling helps lead people to the kingdom of God. The enemy does not want us to experience life with God, nor does he want others to be saved, so we are a threat to his mission on earth. The more we embrace our calling, the more we have the ability to

help lead people to God, aiding in the saving
of souls.

*Why do we need to know who Satan is if
he's already been defeated?*

When you go to war, you must study
your opponent. This is spiritual warfare and
we have a real enemy. Though he has
already lost the war, we still battle against
him in our current lives. Even Jesus had to
encounter and conquer Satan. To know your
enemy is to know who he is… and who he is
not.

The enemy is not the same as God. He
does not hold the same power as God. After
all, he was created by God. God is ruler over
all. God is almighty and victorious. When
combating the enemy, it is important to
remember one thing: the enemy cannot
create anything inside of you, he can only

manipulate and expose what is already there. What does this mean? The enemy does not have the ability to create anything in you. He's not a creator. You've already been created. Perfectly designed by God. With that being said, the enemy knows you. He knows your life and what you've been through. Remember, he roams the earth. But you know what the enemy *really* is? A manipulator.

For example, the enemy cannot create fear in you. But what he can do is manipulate circumstances around you to expose the fear that's already within you. God created your feelings. Fear is a feeling God created in you. Your feelings are to be used for discernment. By manipulating situations and circumstances around you, the enemy can expose the fear you feel towards things you shouldn't fear at all.

The enemy is the ultimate manipulator. The number one tactic used by the enemy is manipulation. Just as he convinced Eve to consume the forbidden fruit, he tried to manipulate Jesus in the desert by tempting him with desires of his flesh. How do you combat manipulation? Boundaries. Walking with God requires you to instill and maintain boundaries.

The more boundaries you surround yourself with, the more you protect yourself. As you set limits to what you will and will not allow in your life, you minimize access for attack. Boundaries protect you. There is a reason God sets expectations for us in His word. These expectations, or limits, are what prevent us from stumbling off the path and being vulnerable to attack.

The enemy is not omnipresent. What does it mean to be omnipresent? It means you can be present everywhere at the same time. God is omnipresent. He can be with you, me, and all of his other children at the same time. The enemy cannot do that. Satan does not have the ability to be in multiple places at a time. Satan himself has identified this in scripture, where he tells God he has been "walking up and down the earth" in the book of Job. Satan is not omnipresent. Does this mean you won't encounter him? Absolutely not. It just means he cannot be in more places than one.

The enemy is not the reason for everything bad in your life. Shocker! Throughout life, I have heard many church goers make statements like "the devil is really coming for me this week" or "the enemy has really been tempting me." But then they will explain their situation. It's something along the lines of "I was short on my rent because I haven't really been to work this week" or "I met someone and we went on a date and I wanted to remain pure but... things just happened." Do these situations sound like they could be the enemy? Sure.

The enemy will absolutely manipulate circumstances in our lives for chaos. That's what he does. That's his agenda. These situations *could* be the enemy. Or... they could just be the temptations of life. Sometimes, we struggle to pay our rent because we didn't work enough hours in the pay period to cover all of our bills. Sounds like a lack of priorities. Sometimes, we give into lust. Sounds like a moment of compromise. The enemy can absolutely attack you. But, if we are honest, he doesn't really have to most of the time. We are pretty good at self-sabotage and giving into our flesh. Here's what the Bible says about temptation:

"The temptations in your life are no different from what others experience. And God is faithful. He will not allow the temptation to be more than you can stand. When you are tempted, he will show you a way out so that you can endure."
(1 Corinthains 10:13 NLT)

The enemy gets a lot of credit for things he doesn't do. When we give him undeserved credit, we give him more authority than he actually has. The Bible tells us that we will encounter trials and hardship. As we encounter these situations, we need to remember that it doesn't necessarily mean we are being attacked by the enemy.

There are situations that happen and moments in our lives that give us an opportunity to assess ourselves. You need to check your heart regularly. Take inventory of what is good and what is bad. If you identify bad, it gives you the ability to remove and release what isn't serving you anymore. How do I know if what's in me is bad? If it produces bad fruit. Let's take a detour from the enemy and talk about the fruits of the spirit.

"But the Holy Spirit produces this kind of fruit in our lives: love, joy, peace, patience, kindness, goodness, faithfulness, gentleness, and self-control. There is no law against these things!"
(Galatians 5:22-23 NLT)

God desires for us to encompass the fruits of the spirit at all times. We are able to do this by being in accordance with God. As you surrender your life for God's calling, your spirit will start to bear fruit. God will help you develop fruits of the spirit through

your walk with Him. If you discover that
there is something in you or something
connected to you that does not resemble the
fruits of the spirit, this can be identified as
"bad fruit." We cannot hold onto bad fruit
and expect it not to impact the good fruit we
are developing with God.

Do you know what happens when one
piece of bad or molded fruit is set next to
healthy fruit? The mold spreads. If we have
bad fruit in our lives, this is generally the
opposite of good fruit, and it can consume
the good fruit we are trying to produce and
maintain. Instead of showing love, we show
hate. Instead of having self-control, we are
undisciplined. Instead of having patience,
we are impatient. Do you know what is
remembered most about a person? The bad
fruit they carry.

It's the reason why you can't remember
every good waitress you've encountered, but

you can sure remember the one bad one.
When we experience something bad in our
lives, we don't want to experience it more
than once. Imagine if somebody encounters
you with bad fruit? Are they going to want
to encounter you again? Probably not. When
we carry bad in our lives, it will impact our
calling from God and the ability to connect
with others.

How do you remove and release what is
bad for you? By giving it to God. By going
to therapy. By surrounding yourself with
community that keeps you accountable. By
avoiding what keeps you connected to the
bad. For example, if you know you struggle
with financial discipline, you may need to
submit to financial mentorship. Ask God
how you can build financial freedom and
take the steps He gives you. Stop going to
places and hanging around people that
encourage you to spend money. All of these

options will help you remove the bad fruit of being undisciplined in your finances.

To remove and release the bad, you have to first identify the bad. And remember that not everything bad is due to the enemy attacking us. Sometimes, it's our own life experiences that have developed the bad in us. But the bad cannot stay. Identifying the bad gives us an opportunity to remove and release it to continue bearing the good fruit God is producing in and through us.

There is so much more that we could learn about the enemy and spiritual warfare. I am not going to do a deep dive into the spiritual realm. That's a topic for another book. What I will do is give you some encouragement: the war is already won. We have victory through Jesus Christ. We have salvation that saves us from hell and gives us everlasting life in heaven with God. Just because we have to encounter the enemy doesn't mean we need to be afraid of Him. Do you know why? The Bible tells us we are able to put on the full armor of God.

What is the armor of God?

The armor of God includes: the belt of truth, breastplate of righteousness, shoes of peace, shield of faith, helmet of salvation, and sword of the spirit (Ephesians 6:10-18). God knew we would encounter the enemy. Remember, this is war. When you walk with God, you must put on the full armor of God. You will need it. Because walking with God saves souls. The enemy is trying to steal, kill, and destroy as many souls as possible, which means you are a target. You are a threat to his mission. But when you walk in the full armor of God, you are covered and protected. The enemy can't manipulate what he can't access. When you do encounter him, you will have everything you need to conquer him. And when trouble arises, you will have the ability to assess whether it is the enemy or something bad within yourself that needs to be dealt with.

THE BEST VERSION OF YOU

This is the part of the story where you expect me to tell you how to be your best self. How to let go of bondage, stop being a hostage, and start living in freedom. Do you know what's funny? God already did that. God gave us salvation.

Salvation is deliverance from sin. That means you are no longer bound by sin. This isn't a free pass to go and commit sin. This is an understanding that God knew we were imperfect, and He loved us so much that He gave us a way out. In a hostage situation, the hostages are looking for a way out. But you have salvation, so you already have a way out. You can't be a hostage to something you have already been saved from.

What does this mean?

To live in the freedom God has given us, you have to be willing to embrace your freedom. If you continue to hold onto bondage, you will keep yourself tied up when God has already set you free. It's like staying in a prison cell when you have been released and asked to leave. And I can already hear your question.

Why would anyone hold onto bondage?

Familiarity. When someone is in bondage, they are enslaved. The greatest example to explain this is through the story

of the Israelites. Let's recap. God freed the
Israelites from Pharaoh's captivity. They
were enslaved to Egypt. God brought them
out of slavery into the wilderness, where
they were to remain before entering the
promised land. God provided them with
protection, nourishment, and instructions for
how to live in the wilderness. He told them
they would conquer any adversary that
would come against them and they would
inhabit the land God set apart for them.

Do you know what the Israelites did?
They complained. They complained about
everything. From the food they were given
to even being in the wilderness. They
created false gods to worship. Yes, you read
that right. God saved them from slavery and
they were worshipping gold statues.
Absolutely insane. There is so much more to
the story, and I encourage you to read it. But
there's a reason I bring up this example. A

big part of why the Israelites struggled so much was out of fear.

Fear? Why would they be afraid? They were rescued by God and promised a land flowing with milk and honey. Sounds like a much better life than being enslaved!

Yes, this is true. But let's place ourselves in their shoes for just a moment. Imagine being led away from everything you have ever known to go somewhere unfamiliar. Imagine not being able to have any control of where you are, what food you will eat, or what will happen to you. I would be afraid too! I would reminisce on what I was familiar with. I would want to go home.

When you live with bondage long enough, it becomes a part of you. It feels like home to you. When you become a new creation in Christ, you are set free from bondage. With that being said, living this life with God is uncomfortable. Relinquishing control is easier said than done. Choosing to walk down a path you know nothing about and sacrificing what you want in life for what God wants for you is a lot harder than it sounds. It takes faith. It takes trust. Often times, we remain in bondage because it is something we feel like we have control over.

What does this mean?

We will allow ourselves to stay captive to traumatic experiences, past hurt, and sin to retain some kind of control in our lives. Here's the thing: what you think you have control of... you don't. God has freed you from bondage, so if you choose not to let it go, you are choosing to be in captivity. Eventually, you will find captivity to be familiar. This familiarity will feel like your safe place. Your home. And it will hinder your ability to walk in your calling and truly experience a relationship with God.

How can you love God and remain in bondage? You can't. This is going to feel heavy. That's because it is. By choosing to be enslaved, you are telling God what you have experienced and what you currently hold onto for control or comfort is more significant than the sacrifice He gave you for freedom. You are decreasing the value of salvation. Minimizing the cost of the blood of Jesus Christ.

Wow, that's a lot.

By choosing to be a hostage, you are choosing to allow the bad to win. That's not supposed to be the outcome of your story. Good conquers evil. God is good. When you allow yourself to be a hostage to the bondage you once had, the cycles you've experienced, or the attacks of the enemy, you are actively keeping yourself from God. It's like saying God's love isn't enough to set you free. As if everything He has done for you is irrelevant. Talk about pain. I can only imagine the heartbreak God has felt watching us choose to be captive to things that hurt us when He has freedom and a promise waiting for us.

I don't want to hurt God.

None of us do. It's never our intention. But it happens. It happens every day. It's in our sinful nature. Sin hurts God. We don't sin to intentionally hurt God. It's not something we can control most of the time. This is why we needed Jesus. This is why we needed salvation. However, when you choose to be a hostage, that is a choice. You are choosing to hurt God. He has already given you freedom. At this point, we know who God is. God is good. God is love. Which means the things He has for us are good and rooted in love. Freedom is good and rooted in love.

If you want to know how to be the best version of yourself, you have to trust God. Trust in His plans, trust in the things He has for you, and trust the path He is leading you down. Every breakthrough is for your good. As you walk with Him, you will develop good fruit. He has given us the ability to put on the full armor of God, and the protection we receive from it is good. We don't have to be afraid because He's already conquered the enemy. He has already given you a way out. Accept His love by embracing the good things He has done for you. Stop being a hostage. You have an exit, use it.

CHAPTER 8

PERFECT TIMING

My car is a 2022 Kia Sportage. The cutest little white SUV you have ever seen. It looks small from the outside, but boy, does that baby have space! She's fast as a whip and I named her Deborah. Why? I don't know, because I really like the name Deborah. I call her Lil Debbie for short… I know, hysterical. One day, I was driving to school and my tire light came on. Because this is a newer car, it has a safety feature that shows me which tire is the problem. It said my right front tire was low on air. Sounds like a simple fix, right?

This car was less than a year old at the time, so there was no reason it should have any issues. The tires were practically brand new. Being concerned for Lil Debbie, I drove to the nearest Firestone to have someone look at the tire in question. The man who examined it put air in my tire and let me know that he was able to visibly see a nail, but it shouldn't be of concern since my tire was not deflated or losing air quickly. He said to bring the car by after school and he could patch it right up for me. Glory to God! I rushed to school as I was now running behind schedule.

Just as I was turning the corner to the street my school was located on, I hit a pothole on the right side of my car, causing the nail to fully deflate my tire. I carefully pulled into the school parking lot and parked in a spot that would be accessible to a tow truck. I knew there was no way I would get that car to a shop without some help. Now, when you are ballin' on a teacher budget, every penny counts. However, today was the perfect day for this to happen as it was payday. Not only did I make it to school on time, but I was able to have my car towed to get a new tire and I had the money in my account to take care of it right away. No rim damage, nothing affecting my classes, everything lined up. Perfect timing!

Our God is an "on-time" God. He has perfect timing. Though we may not see it in every situation, He is already working it out for our good. What does this mean? When God calls you to something, He calls you at exactly the right time. He has already factored in every part of you. Even the parts you are still working on. He knows you. He knows what you struggle with, He knows where your heart is, He knows you better than you know yourself. Our calling is not about us, but it is for us. God calls us at just the right time.

DECLINING THE CALL

My biggest pet peeve is when my phone rings and I can clearly see I am receiving a spam call. Drives me nuts! Why are you calling me? How did you get this number? No, I do not want to talk to you about my car's extended warranty. LEAVE. ME. ALONE. I am hitting the decline button on that call faster than it has time to reach my voicemail. Why? Because I'm not interested. The same goes for me if I am receiving a call from someone I know, but I'm not in the mood to talk to you. In my mind, it doesn't mean I don't love you; I just cannot handle your call right now.

Here's the thing. When God calls you, He calls you at a specific time for a specific reason. It may not be about you, but it is for you. Your calling uses you to reach people, but it also impacts your life for the better.

Walking in your calling gives you the ability to experience God's love and blessings in ways you couldn't without Him. However. Every call has an expiration date. Just like the calls we receive every day, God will call you to different people, places, and things at different times. All of this is connected to His purpose for your life.

What does this mean?

It means we have a choice. Let's go back to the discussion of free will. If I see an incoming call from my mom and I decline that call, I am actively choosing not to speak with her. The Bible tells us that God knocks on the door of our hearts every day, and we have a choice on whether we will let Him in or leave Him at the door knocking. When God calls you, you have a choice on whether you will accept that call or decline it. Please understand that when you decline a call from God, you are not just hindering yourself, you are hindering the people God wants you to impact for the kingdom. Your time to accept the call is limited.

Have you ever been overdue on a bill? You only receive so many opportunities to pay that bill before they stop calling you to pay it and send it to collections. God will give you so many opportunities to answer a call before that opportunity is missed. And yes, you can miss an opportunity from God. Does He know you are going to miss it? Yes He does. Will He allow you to miss it? Yes He will. Why? Because He loves you enough to let you choose what you will and will not experience in this life.

He also allows you to choose whether or not you will be used by Him. Everything in this life is a choice. Just remember, every decision ends in reward or consequence. By choosing to decline a call from God, you are choosing to reap the consequence of missing that call, which could impact God's ability to use you for other opportunities in the future.

SENT TO VOICEMAIL

When I call someone and they do not answer my call, I will leave them a voicemail to let them know I called. This is pretty customary for most people. If it is someone special to me, it is usually a goofy and heartfelt message asking them to call me back and telling them how much I love them. If it is a job or someone who is more of an acquaintance to me, the message I leave usually holds more of a professional tone. Nonetheless, I will still leave a message to let you know I called and what I called for, leaving little hints of the importance of my call to you. That is only if your voicemail is not full though. If your voicemail is full, I don't have an opportunity to leave you a message, even if I want to.

Just as declining a call from God can hinder us, so can delaying a call. Again, God calls us at the right time. The perfect time. If we send the call to voicemail, that means we are asking God to leave a message with what He is needing from us and we will get back to Him as soon as we are available. That leaves room for disaster.

Here's an example. Imagine your mom is calling you to let you know that she saw on the news there was an emergency situation happening in your neighborhood and you need to lock your doors and be on alert. You send the call to voicemail and decide you will listen to it later. You put on your running shoes, slip on your headphones, and go for a jog. You are now vulnerable to the danger in your area because you missed the warning she was trying to give you.

Now imagine God is calling you because He needs you to transition out of a situation urgently. You sent God to voicemail, meaning, you can hear Him giving you warnings, and you can visibly see the signs He is showing you, but you do not allow His discernment to guide you. You are not readily available to Him. Now, you are experiencing something dangerous to you because you did not heed His warnings or truly accept His instructions at the time He gave them.

What does it mean to send God to voicemail?

It means that we only allow God to speak to us when we want to hear His voice. We choose when we want to listen to what He has to say. It's at this time when we decide if we are ready or if this is something we find important to us. This type of relationship with God is known as transactional. When you have a relationship with God that is transactional, it is one-sided. You only speak to God when you want or need something, but when He wants to call you to something or speak with you about something, you are not readily available to Him.

Could you imagine if your best friend treated you like you were transactional? Every time you called, they sent you to voicemail and they only ever called back when it seemed like something they were interested in or could benefit from? What a gross feeling. Same goes for when we hear

God giving us instructions or see His signs for us, but we do not act right away as we are deciding whether or not this is something we are interested in or could benefit from.

God is our father. He also calls us friend. A relationship goes two ways, whether you are partners or friends. You cannot love someone and only choose to show them love when you feel like it. Love is a choice. Love is an action. When we love someone, we will choose them over ourselves.

"Love is patient and kind. Love is not jealous or boastful or proud or rude. It does not demand its own way. It is not irritable, and it keeps no record of being wronged. It does not rejoice about injustice but rejoices whenever the truth wins out. Love never gives up, never loses faith, is always

hopeful, and endures through every
circumstance."
(1 Corinthians 13:4-7 NLT)

God is patient. He will not demand His own way with you. He won't give up on you either. He wants to be with you. That's why He created you. That includes talking to you. Guiding you. Directing and protecting you. God wants YOU. If you only make yourself available to God when you feel like you're ready, how much do you really love God? Is that *really* love?

What does love have to do with your
calling?

It's simple: You cannot actively love someone you choose to ignore or avoid. You cannot truly love someone if you only want to benefit from them without connecting with them. There is never going to be an opportunity God calls you to that is not important. You have to know that God's timing is perfect to know how important every call is. There is something He wants you to learn or someone He wants you to reach. The call has a reason. And every reason is connected to purpose.

If you send God to voicemail, you are denying the importance of His call at the time He is calling you. This is dismissing His good plans for you. His plans are to show you how much He loves you. His plans are for your future. His plans are to give you hope. To truly appreciate the importance of the calling He has for you is to understand the love He has for you.

As you walk with God, start evaluating how often you allow God to speak to you. Think about how often you spend time in worship. When you pray, are you asking

God for all the things you want more than you thank him for all He has already done? When was the last time you allowed yourself to sit in His presence without expectation of a blessing or miracle? Without asking Him for something?

It is in our selfish nature to focus on ourselves more than others, including God. When we choose God and the calling He places on our lives, we are laying down ourselves for more of Him. We are choosing to love Him. This is our purpose in life. To be with God. To trust God. To follow God. And doing these things shows how much we truly love God.

AIRPLANE MODE

In chapter 2, I mentioned airplane mode, and I said we would talk about it later. Well… Houston, we have landed! This is the scariest thing we can do in our walk with God. Airplane mode and Do Not Disturb are arguably the most commonly used settings in today's world. Why is this? Because we don't want to be bothered. Putting your phone on Do Not Disturb doesn't shut you off to the world as much as airplane mode does, but it still hinders your ability to receive messages and phone calls at the time they are coming in. This gives you a sense of peace and control as you can go throughout your day without being interrupted.

I have added Do Not Disturb in this section because of how similar it is, however, in my opinion, it's also relative to declining a call or sending it to voicemail. With Do Not Disturb, there is still an option to leave a voicemail or, if a call is urgent, call twice to get through to someone. The voicemail notification will show on your phone without making a sound or disrupting you. With airplane mode, you do not have that luxury. When a phone is on airplane mode, it prevents any incoming text messages or calls from coming through. A voicemail can be sent, but you will not receive a notification that it is there. The setting was designed to protect your phone while traveling at high altitudes on flights. I have used the setting on my phone to give myself a break from receiving any contact from anyone whatsoever, as I'm sure others can relate. Airplane mode allows you to coast.

What does it mean to "coast?"

It means you are able to go through your day without any notifications. It blocks any ability to be reached. When you are coasting, you are directly focused on yourself and doing what it is that you would like to do without being disturbed. When we put our life on airplane mode, we block God out completely. This is when we start walking in the way we want to walk and we start choosing things we want rather than following the instructions God has for us. We live our lives completely oblivious because we have shut off God's ability to give us discernment. He can't reach us.

Once airplane mode is turned off, all of the notifications you were supposed to receive start coming in. It takes your phone a second to adjust to being available again, but once it does, your phone is going off the wall with every update, text message, phone call, email. It shows you everything you missed. When you are coasting through life, you are missing opportunities God has for you. And it is not until you stop coasting and open yourself back up to the Lord that you realize what you have missed out on.

This is why we must stay connected to God. We cannot walk through life making decisions for ourselves. We are not even supposed to do life by ourselves. The first thing God said was not good was for man to be alone. We are vulnerable to doing things and making decisions that will hurt us. We were created by God for God. We were created to need God. I don't know about you, but every decision I have ever made for myself outside of God has always ended in misery. From draining my bank account to dating the wrong person to choosing the wrong place to work. The list of my life mistakes is a long one.

I'm sure you have experienced times in your life where you have coasted and done things on your own, thinking you were making good decisions, only to find yourself

in desperate need of God's help. We have all
been there. Do you know what the coolest
thing about God is? That He loves us so
much that he sent Jesus to wipe the slate
clean. He is the ultimate example of love as
He does not keep record of wrongdoings.
We can come to God, repent, and turn away
from our mistakes, surrendering to His will.
And He will welcome us with open arms.
Not because we deserve it, but because He
loves us. Because that's who He is. It all
goes back to love.

No matter what opportunities you have
missed in the past, God can still use you in
the future. You just need to make sure you
are available to him. That is what it is all
about. Being ready for the call. You may not
feel ready, but you will be ready, because
God always calls us at the right time. We
can trust that we are ready to walk in our
calling because God's timing is always

perfect. If you want to be used by God or are waiting for His call, stay focused on Him and His word. When the time is right, God will direct your steps.

CHAPTER 9

SOLID FOUNDATION

One thing about moving a lot is getting used to inhabiting a new house. It takes a minute to get familiar with each room and feel comfortable in the space you now live in. Moving is a lot of work! From unloading and unpacking all of your belongings to hanging up pictures and making your house feel like a home. With every move we made growing up, we learned how to downsize. My mom would pack the essentials and have us go through our belongings to decide what we thought we could not live without. We could only take limited items with us. Everything else was either donated or thrown away.

Somehow, we would acquire so much more than we previously had in our other homes. When moving time came again, we would repeat the process. Today, I have found comfort in a minimal lifestyle because I could not grow an attachment to belongings. I still find myself going through my belongings regularly and deciding whether it is really a priority to have them or if I should get rid of them. This made moving across the country easy for me.

Remember when I told you about the 21 Days of Prayer and Fasting I did with Transformation Church back in 2019? Well, I left a pretty important detail out. There was one thing God kept saying to me through that entire three-week prayer fest. God told me I would be moving from Oklahoma to Arizona. At this point in my life, I had just rededicated my life to God four months prior. My life was an absolute mess!

I was sleeping on my mom's couch, I didn't have a stable job, and I definitely didn't have money to move across the country. What was God thinking? It is now 2024, and I can confidently say that I not only live in Arizona, but I have my own place, I have a company of my own, and have stable income. God is so cool!

Back to the story. He told me this in 2019. When He called me to Arizona, I didn't exactly know what the plan was, but I knew that if He really wanted me there, He would make it happen. From that moment until the day I left Oklahoma, my heart longed to be somewhere else. I don't know how to explain this to you in any other way but this: I knew I wasn't where I should be.

There were moments where I started looking at jobs in Colorado, so I could be near my siblings and nephews there. I looked at moving to neighboring states like Texas and Missouri. I even looked into moving to Florida, because who wouldn't want to wake up on the beach every day? I didn't really know if Arizona is where I would end up, but I knew I couldn't stay where I was.

Now, we all experienced 2020, so I don't have to tell you how hard and devastating that year was. The isolation and quarantine impacted everyone in such a hard way. Our society still hasn't fully recovered. With that being said, God provided stable income through that entire year. I was able to work from home and remain consistent in making money and working overtime.

I lived with a roommate who I also worked with. We were both taking classes trying to better our lives. This was also the year I started my master's degree. I knew I needed to go back to teaching in a classroom. I missed being a music teacher and felt lost in the career path I was currently in. I knew I wasn't where I should be.

In December 2020, I did an interview for a music teaching position with a district I was referred to by one of my close friends. She worked for this district and knew I would be an amazing fit. She gave me a glowing recommendation and the school called me for an interview. To say I was excited is an understatement! This was also the worst interview I've ever experienced for a job. There were over eight people present in this room besides me and at least half of them looked too bored to care.

Now, I do not understand why some school districts do this, but that seems highly excessive to incorporate so many faculty members in one interview. Moving on. The interview was so bad that the principal and vice principal both pulled their phones out and were texting in the middle of a line of

questioning between another faculty
member and myself. I had never felt so
intimidated or defeated. Leaving the school
parking lot, I just couldn't help but
breakdown. I was sobbing uncontrollably
and finally looked at the sky and said:

"I don't understand, God. I know this is
what I'm supposed to do. I know I'm a good
teacher and a good person. When is life
going to be different? Why does it have to
be this way?"

Do you know what God said to me? He
responded with:

**"When are you going to do things
MY way?"**

OUCH. I had been walking with God
for a little over two years at this point. I

served with the church, stayed connected to godly community, and thought I was doing a good job at being a Christian woman. It was in that moment that I realized I was trying to do what only God could do. I was trying to make my plans work instead of His.

See, if you could do everything on your own, you would never need God. If you could make everything happen yourself, you would never see God as the loving father He is and you would start to identify as your own savior. God needed me to relinquish control. God needed me to truly let go and have faith in Him to fulfill His plans. To be my solid foundation.

WHERE TO START

This lit a fire in my soul! I wanted His plans for me, and I wanted to trust Him with

my life. It was in this moment that I made
the decision to lay down my way and do it
His way. But there was just one problem...
what was HIS way? I knew there were
things He was gravitating me towards, such
as being back in a classroom and leaving
Oklahoma, I just didn't know how to get
there. It was like starting at the beginning of
a book and skipping the middle to read the
last chapter. I knew the general consensus of
what He wanted for me and what the
ultimate goal was, I just didn't understand
the whole plan or process of how to walk it
out.

Let's back up to our starting line. Do
you remember where your calling starts? It
starts with accepting the call. BUT. Do you
remember what you must do before you get
to the starting line? If you said, " build a
deeper relationship with God," you nailed it!
Developing a real relationship with God is

where it all starts. God can't call you to the life He has for you if He can't trust you to stay with him and do it His way. You know when a parent buys their child a car for their 16th birthday? The average parent looks for a vehicle that will protect their child and be feasible for them to drive and take care of.

Now, parents don't generally hand car keys to a child that has not successfully passed their driving test. Once the child crosses the threshold of being a licensed driver, that is when a parent can trust them with their own vehicle. Remember when I said your life with God is like a car? Guess what, I wasn't joking. God cannot hand you the keys to the life He has for you without being able to trust that it is something that you can handle.

He would not be a good father if He gave you an opportunity to be reckless. That's not in His nature. God is love. And

He created you out of love. He wants good things for you because He loves you. That includes your protection. He will never give you something He knows you are not ready for. This doesn't mean He won't give us things we cannot handle by ourselves.

When I say He will never give you something He knows you are not ready for, I mean that He will not set you up for failure. His plans for your life require your trust and faith in Him. He must be at the center of all that you do. Your solid foundation. His calling for your life requires you to be connected to Him because those plans are connected to His purpose for you. You cannot fulfill your calling without God.

THINGS HAPPEN WHEN YOU PRAY

Why Me, God?

Learning the plan and understanding what needed to be done in order to fulfill all that God had for me took sacrifice. The next couple of weeks, God asked me to do things that were out of my comfort zone, like give my last $20 to the crazy faith offering at TC. Stuff that I would have to completely trust Him to do. The more time I spent in His word and in worship, the stronger I felt. I made the decision that on New Year's Eve, I would stay up the entire night in worship. I wanted to be with God and go into the new year in His presence. What I did not know was the breakthrough that would happen from that decision.

On NYE entering into 2021, God started revealing His calling for my life. He took me back to 2019, when He said I would move to Arizona. I knew I needed to organize the calling. I cut strips of paper, wrote down everything God said to believe

Him for, and taped them up. These were displayed in our living room, so not only could my roommate and I see them, but anyone who came over could read them as well. I called it my "prayer wall."

After writing every part of the plan and posting it on the wall, I ended my night in prayer and worship. As I was turning off the worship music and getting ready to go to sleep, God said so clearly:

"Don't stop praying. If you believe me for it, I will do it."

Don't stop praying. Three simple words. One powerful sentence. We know that prayer is what directly connects us to God. It is the most powerful tool we have as human beings, and we are able to utilize prayer to open the floodgates of heaven and release blessings. Praying sounds easy enough right? Or is it. The Bible is very specific on how we should pray (Luke 11:1-4). The Bible also explains what happens when we pray (Phillipians 4:6-7).

By thanking God for everything He has done, you are acknowledging that He is the one who takes care of you. You are showing gratitude and love to our King of Kings and Lord of Lords. Prayer without gratitude is null and void. God wants relationship with us. We know that relationship cannot be transactional. God is not a genie. You don't rub the Bible, ask Him for 3 blessings, and go about your merry way. It requires sacrifice. Sacrifice is an act of love. And love is a choice.

By asking God for what you need, you are acknowledging His power. You are exercising your faith muscle. This is relinquishing control from trying to create your own way and asking God to show you

how to do it His way. This is how we show
God we trust Him. When you pray, you are
bringing yourself to God in submission.

One of the hardest things we can do in
life is ask for help. This is because our world
has made us feel as though asking for help is
wrong. The world has taught us that we
should be self-sufficient. But where in the
Bible does it say that you should be self-
sufficient? Where does it say that you
should rely on you, and only you, to take
care of yourself? Breaking news: that's not
in there.

God has called each and every one of us
to rely on His strength for everything that
we need. He has instructed us to be generous
givers and help each other. We are to serve
and love one another. We know that God
never intended for us to be alone. He
intended for us to care for each other and
steward well over what He blesses us with.

What gives God the ability to bless us?
Prayer.

If we never ask God for the things that
we need, He cannot intercede. If we never
bring our lives to God and ask Him for His
blessings, He can't bless us. You can't
receive help if it's not known you need help.
And just like love is a choice, so is trust.
You must choose to trust God by asking
Him for what you need through prayer and
He will always take care of you.

Prayer is our way of connecting to God.
It is our way of preserving our solid
foundation. Giving God gratitude for all He
has done and submitting our desires and life
to Him shows our love for Him. It shows
God we are willing to sacrifice our own
ways for His. This is what keeps us
stabilized throughout our calling. He is our
solid foundation, and He cannot be moved.

CHAPTER 10

HERE'S MY WORSHIP

January 2021: I couldn't have been more on fire for the Lord! My prayer wall was loaded with everything God had in store for me, and I wasn't going to miss a single opportunity! I worked hard and built a solid routine. This was going to be MY year!

February 2021: I stayed diligent in prayer, reading my Bible, and spending time with God. Spirit still on fire. Life was moving along just fine. Kept working hard and pushing on. God is good!

March 2021: Still praying. Still believing God. Things are still the same, but I'm keeping my faith. Started looking outside of Oklahoma for places to move.

Started applying for new jobs. I know He is
with me.

<u>April 2021</u>: I got a new job with
unlimited overtime and feeling pretty good!
Not working as a music teacher yet, but
that's okay. Honestly, life is better. The best
it's been in a long time. Started tithing and
paying off debts. Started going to the gym
and started losing weight. Still spending
time with God and keeping up with prayer.

Life was moving along and things
seemed to get better and better every day. I
was eating better, sleeping better, and more
joyful. It really felt like everything was
falling into place - then it happened. I felt
this strong tug on my heart. I had just started
a brand new, really good job, but I wasn't
working as a music teacher. It was time to
start applying to schools again. After all,

being a music teacher was on the prayer wall, so what did I have to lose?

I must have submit my resume to dozens of schools across Oklahoma, and even submit some applications in Colorado, where some of my family lived.

Then the strangest thing happened. I came across a job posting for a music teacher... in Arizona. It was a listing that popped up while I was searching through Colorado jobs. Just one lonely listing. Totally different state. Totally random. In my eyes anyways.

"That's weird... I wasn't really looking in Arizona. But God did say I was going to live there someday. Ehh. What's the harm in applying?"

I submitted my application and didn't think twice about it. Honestly, with all the other schools I applied for, I'd probably be working for a school in Oklahoma soon anyways... or so I thought. I didn't hear anything back from any of the schools I applied for in Oklahoma, so I just kept working my current job and praying. A little over a week later, I received an email from HR to do a preliminary phone interview for a school I applied for... in Arizona.

"Wait WHAT? I must have applied to over 20 schools in Oklahoma alone. Why is the only one I have heard from in... Arizona?"

I couldn't help but feel confused. That is until I went back to my prayer wall. I read through every single thing I had written on the wall. That's when I came across one piece of paper I had overlooked. It read:

"Prepare for the big move."

I forgot all about this. I pulled it off the wall and stared at it. That's when I noticed writing on the backside of the paper. It read:

"… to Arizona."

"Now wait just a minute. God… WHAT? Everything in life is finally starting to feel like it is falling into place. I've got good money coming in, I'm paying off debts, taking care of my health. I have a good thing going here. Just you and me. And now you want to move me… to ARIZONA? That can't be right."

And you know what God said:

"It's time."

That's all He said. That's all I got. I sat there in utter disbelief. Just as I was finally starting to feel like life was on the right track, here I am, staring this little piece of paper in the face, having to cope with the idea of moving… to Arizona. I decided to trust God and remain in prayer.

"If this is your plan, you will make a way. I trust you."

THE CHOICE IS YOURS

The phone interview with HR went really well. In fact, it was the best conversation I've ever had with a school district. The level of confidence I had going into the process was something I had never felt before. Writing this is funny to me now as I look back on this moment. At the time, I couldn't understand why everything felt so... right. Of course it did... it was God's plan all along!

I received an email from HR that same week letting me know that the principal and vice principal of the school I applied for would like to do a second interview virtually. How exciting! That interview went great. So great, in fact, that I was given an offer letter to work there shortly after. Things were moving quickly. But before the offer letter came from my school in Arizona, I received a phone call from another school in Oklahoma. This school was right down the street from my apartment. They expressed how impressed with my résumé they were and how they wanted me to come in for an interview the following week. This was a school I was very interested in working for.

"Umm… okay wait a minute. Now I have TWO schools to worry about?! I thought I was supposed to go to Arizona. I'm so confused."

I needed an answer. I prayed and kept getting the same response from God:

"It's time."

"It's time for WHAT? Which option? What am I supposed to do?"

I've given you a lot of my testimony here. There is a reason for this, I promise. This part of my life was the first real moment that I had to decide. The first opportunity God showed me was part of my calling. The second opportunity was a distraction. When God calls you to something, you will always have an opportunity to choose something different than what He calls you to. Your calling from God is never going to feel comfortable. But the option to choose outside of your calling will.

Walking in your calling is choosing to walk a path led by God. You are choosing to take steps that you wouldn't take on your own. There's a reason it's called the road less traveled. This is where the choice is made clear. When we talk about preparing to accept a call, we talk about building a relationship with God. This means reading your Bible, spending time in God's presence, and consistently praying. We know how powerful the word of God is, and we have explored in detail the significance of prayer and how it can impact our lives. The last thing we need to examine is the importance of spending time in God's presence. In other words, the importance of worship.

If you are going to have a deep relationship with God, you need to know how to worship Him. It's not enough to read your Bible and pray. Those two things are key to building and maintaining your relationship with the Lord and being able to walk in the direction He calls you. However, without understanding and implementing worship, you will lack the ability to fully acknowledge and love Him. Without worship, you cannot fully surrender your own desire for His plans.

What does it mean to "worship?"

To worship something is to express devotion and adoration. Another way of explaining worship is to honor. Honor is having high respect for something. When you worship God, you are expressing respect for Him. Do you know what respect is? It is a feeling of deep admiration. The definition of the words adore, admire, reverence, and honor all encompass two similar words. The first word: respect. To worship God is to show respect to Him.

How do you show respect to God?

The same way you would show respect to your earthly parents. Let me explain. If my mom asked me to do something, let's say she needed me to help her clean her house, even now as an adult, I would do it. Why? Because she's my mom. Everything she has done for me in my life, everything she's sacrificed to give me the life that I have today, and the love she has shown me is more than enough for me to set aside time to do what she asked me to do.

To show God respect is to do what He asks you to do. What is the first step when walking in your calling? Obedience. To show God respect is to be obedient to the things He has asked you to do. When you walk in obedience, you are showing God that His sacrifice to give us salvation and the love He has for us is more than enough.

The second word: love. We know from the book of 1 Corinthians how God feels about love. But do you know the definition of love? To love is to feel deep affection. Another word used in place of affection is admiration. Are we seeing a trend here? So, let's put the two together. To worship God is to love and respect Him. In other words, to worship God is to feel and show admiration for Him.

God doesn't just want you to do things out of obligation. Because you know it's the "right" thing to do. He wants you to do what

He asks because you admire Him so much that your heart longs for Him. He wants you to pursue Him. To know Him. To love Him. To respect Him. You can't worship something you don't admire.

There will always be an opportunity to choose outside of what God wants for you. Our world is full of opportunities to walk in darkness. What I love about God is that He knew we were imperfect. He knew we would stumble, but He loves us enough to hold us by the hand and help us keep walking (Psalm 37:24). When an opportunity comes along that can take you off the path of your calling, you have a choice. But the choice isn't whether or not you will do the right thing. The choice is whether or not you admire God enough to do what He asks. That is the true heart of worship.

GET YOU A SHARYL

My first time joining a group through TC, I was a nervous wreck. I had never been part of a church group and I had a past I was not proud of. There was still lingering insecurity from my childhood. A lot of past traumas from toxic relationships. I had no idea what to expect. But I went. I wanted to connect with women who were walking with God because I wanted to know how to walk with Him too. Having a relationship with God was new to me. I was never taught how to really have a relationship with God as a child. I needed help.

That night, standing in the Panera Bread parking lot, I contemplated going inside. I'm so glad I did. Because that night, I met Sharyl. Sharyl was new to the church and had just moved to Tulsa from the great state of Kentucky, where chicken is not a rarity.

Let's all laugh together. Sharyl was very calm, down to earth, and easy to talk to. She was warm and kind. The first real friend I ever had in the church. That's my girl still today. When I say everyone needs a Sharyl, I mean it. But not my Sharyl, she has her hands full.

As I grew my relationship with God, Sharyl was there. She and I committed to doing the 21 Days of Prayer and Fasting together back in 2019, and she actually did the fasting part (proud of you, pumpkin). She witnessed that school call me after the prayer session. She was the first person I told that God wanting me to move to Arizona. And you know what this girl said?

"Sweet! When are you leaving?"

Sister… WHAT? Anyways. She witnessed many big moments in my walk

with God. From getting baptized to serving
with the church. New jobs, new homes, and
new life experiences. Sharyl also witnessed
many difficult moments in my life. She
welcomed me with open arms and loved me
so much. She prayed with me, counseled
me, and even gave me a couch to sleep on
when I had nowhere to go. Her
accountability and genuine love for me are
why I'm here. I will never be able to thank
her enough for all she has helped me grow
through. God knew I needed Sharyl.

Let's go back to the moment I had to
decide between these two jobs. I was
conflicted. I knew what God said, but this
was scary. What He was asking me to do
was not only uncomfortable, but life
changing. My brain was contemplating
every possible outcome, both good and bad.
I didn't know what to do. I did the only
thing that felt right: I called Sharyl. As I'm

explaining my current situation, she cuts me short and asks a very simple question:

"What does God want you to do?"

I stopped for a moment, contemplating how to answer. I wanted to word this in a way that would answer her question while also aiding my own feelings and insecurities. Before I could give her the articulate response thought up in my mind, she followed up:

" Emily, God told you about this move to Arizona years ago. Now, God is giving you the opportunity that He told you He would, so you need to make the right decision. And you know what the right decision is. It's time."

It's time. I had heard those words before. It is exactly what God said to me. I had the exact confirmation I needed on the decision that I needed to make.

Why are you telling us this?

There is a reason God said it is not good for man to be alone. While Adam had God always, he needed a partner. Helpmate. Community. Had I not been connected to Sharyl, a person also walking with the Lord, I would not have had the accountability I needed and may have taken the advice of my family and other friends not walking with God, who all said the same thing:

"Are you nuts? There is nothing in Arizona for you. Everything you need is here. You have a good job, a nice place to

live, and life is good. You don't need to
move. Stay where you are."

Without Sharyl, I would've never taken
the leap of faith to trust God and move to
Arizona. I wouldn't have my company, my
friends, or my home. All of the amazing
things I have witnessed and experienced
would've never happened. My relationship
with God wouldn't be even close to where it
is today, and if you ask anyone that knows
me, they will tell you God is my everything.

The truth is: this book wouldn't even
exist. God told me I was going to write this
book in November of 2021. AFTER I had
already moved to Arizona. My life would be
drastically different. Thank God for His
good plans and the community He knew I
needed. This is the power of community. To
have people in your life who you are equally
yoked with.

What does it mean to be "equally yoked?"

This means you have people in your life that have the same desire to chase after God that you do. There is a reason why God wants our relationships to be equally yoked. When you are connected to people who are not walking the same pace with God that you are, or they do not have the same level of faith or foundation with God that you do, these people can potentially hinder your calling.

People that are not equally yoked with you will not be able to support, counsel, or lead you in your calling because they will not have the level of understanding they need to keep up with you. One of the most common examples I can give you is Christians dating. If you are a man or a woman who believes in God, generally, the church encourages you to meet someone else who also goes to the same type of church as you. And that's cute. But denomination does not automatically mean you are equally yoked. Let's look at some examples.

If I date a man who believes that prayer is optional, but I believe prayer is the foundation of my walk with God, we are not equally yoked. If I date a man who doesn't believe in tithing, but I do, we are not equally yoked. If I date a man who is willing to have sex outside of marriage, but I take my vow of purity very seriously, we are not equally yoked. There are dozens of examples I could continue with, but I think you get the point. While there is nothing wrong with knowing someone you are unequally yoked with, there is a difference between being associated with someone and doing life together.

Relationships are simple. To be in a relationship is to be connected to someone. That's the whole definition. Connection. You can have a relationship with literally anyone. If you connect with someone, you've built a relationship with them. For a person walking with God, having equally yoked relationships is critical. To connect with someone is not enough. We need to connect with someone on the same level of faith as us. When you build a relationship with someone who is not at the same level of faith as you, there are areas of your walk with God you are leaving vulnerable to compromise. There are three types of relationships:

- Discipleship
- Mentorship
- Friendship

God will connect us with people throughout our life. Your calling is not about you, it is about others. This means you will encounter people throughout your walk with God that He wants you to connect with. How He wants you to connect with these people is what you have to figure out. This is why you must have a deep relationship with God before knowing and accepting your calling. Without God's discernment, you will mistake your role in a person's life, which can drastically influence your calling and life.

People who we often identify as being in discipleship with us are our church community. These are people after God's own heart. People, just like you, who want to grow closer to God every day, walk in His calling for them, and walk with other believers doing the same thing. This type of community can be meaningful and personal.

The primary focus of discipleship always goes back to God.

Walking with others in discipleship is learning how to love God with one another and leading each other closer to Him. It's all focused around being a follower of Christ. Anyone can fall within the category of discipleship. Remember what your purpose on this earth is? To make disciples of God's people. Who are God's people? Everyone. You have the ability to be a disciple to any person you come in contact with. This means you are able to talk about God and the salvation He gave us through Jesus with anyone.

You may encounter people who do not know God or have just recently given their life to God. These individuals will also fall under the category of discipleship. This is your opportunity as a disciple of Christ to help lead them closer to God. To support and counsel them using God's word and His discernment. It means helping others follow God as He desires for all.

Mentorship is slightly different. When a person falls under the category of mentorship, it is for one of two reasons: you are mentoring them or they are mentoring you. It's important to understand the difference between discipling and mentoring. Discipling is specifically helping guide or lead one another closer to God. Mentoring is a little bit more specific. A mentor still helps guide and direct someone, but with a specific focus. This could be in your career, health, finances, and so on. A mentor will lead you towards specific goals and objectives. They work with you on building set skills needed for your walk with God.

To have a friendship is to have a relationship with someone that you are affectionate about. In other words, it is to connect with someone that you admire. How do we worship God again? Through admiration. Why do you think He calls us friend? It all connects. When you develop a friendship, you develop admiration towards an individual you have connected with. You love and respect this person. This is also the foundation of marriage. Two friends build on the admiration they have for one another. The deeper your relationship grows; the more love develops. This is why it is said that your spouse is your best friend. Why do you think we are called the bride of Christ? Is your mind blown yet?

Our relationships here on earth are supposed to mimic our relationship with God. However, let's not get confused. God is above all things. He is the head and not the tail. He is Alpha and Omega. He is the beginning and the end. What this means is, we cannot place anything above Him. Our relationship with God should be the most important thing in our life. He comes first. Who you are connected to is a close second. If you are not careful, your relationships will start to become idolized.

This is why you must spend time with God. And this is why being equally yoked is so important. Those with the same desire to follow God will always point you towards Him and not themselves. If your relationship focuses more on a person than God, you may need to rethink that relationship. God will never bring someone into your life that takes you from Him. This doesn't mean you won't encounter people that you are unequally yoked with. It leads back to choice. Do you love God enough to separate from those who take you from Him? That is a question you have to answer yourself.

Our worship to God is putting Him above anything else. To do as He asks because we love and respect Him. He comes first. Next comes our community. The relationships we build on earth follow after our relationship with God. Another way we worship God is by carefully maintaining and stewarding well over our relationships with others.

God will lead you to your community. He will bring people into your life that He knows you need. You will also encounter others you don't need. This is why we need God's discernment. He wants us to make each other better. Make each other stronger. And lead one another closer to Him. Let's help one another keep our eyes fixed on God.

CHAPTER 11

ARE WE THERE YET?

Moving across state lines as a kid is always an adventure. When we would move, we didn't fly and we didn't have movers. Our family would pack everything up, load the moving truck, and road trip to our new home. Oddly enough, this is my preferred method of moving today. Effective, but time-consuming. I still love a good road trip! So much to see and experience.

Little Emily, however, wasn't always enthusiastic about the long drives. My mom had a schedule. She wanted us to get there as soon as possible and she did not want to stop for anything. This meant long hours in a cramped car with my other siblings. Talk about an uncomfortable nightmare! We didn't stop unless mom needed to get gas or we got food. These stops were not long either. Do what you got to do and get back in the car.

It would be hours into the drive and I would have the same question in my mind throughout the entire trip:

"Are we there yet?"

I just wanted to get out of the car. Breathing in fresh air, stretching out, and enjoying freedom! Before that could happen, we had to get there. It was a long process. One I never enjoyed. But it was the only way to get to our new home. And once we arrived, everyone was grateful for it to be over.

In your walk with God, throughout your calling, you will experience what is known as a "waiting season." Your waiting season is going to feel like you are stuck. Like you are stagnant. Almost like you are walking on a treadmill. Moving, but staying in the same place. You know you're putting in work, you can feel the results of the work you're putting in, but you haven't gone anywhere and there's no end in sight. Seasons of waiting are never fun.

There are similar seasons of life that feel like waiting seasons. These are seasons we experience pain in. These are known as heartbreak seasons. A heartbreak season will feel like a season of waiting, but often times involves pain you must heal from. This can be anything that breaks your heart. Both seasons can be equally exhausting. When you encounter a waiting season or a heartbreak season, there is one thing to remember: there is always a reason.

Regardless of what you encounter, God always has a reason for it. Whether He wants to expose something in you, heal

different parts of you, or stretch your faith.
To build faith, you have to put it to use. If
you never experienced situations that
required faith, you would never need faith.
If you never needed faith, you would never
need God.

Faith is the key to making it through a
waiting or heartbreak season. You must
have faith that God will fulfill His promises
and get you to the other side. But waiting is
part of the process. Your calling is on God's
time. Not yours. As much as we might not
like waiting, it is necessary for us to
experience. It's in the waiting that we
experience the biggest breakthroughs.

Waiting seasons bring many questions,
thoughts, and feelings. These are valid but
should not take us off the path of our calling.
Neither should the pain we experience in our
heartbreak seasons. How we handle these
seasons is connected to the people, places,

and things God has for us in our calling. So, get comfortable. You might be here a while.

TIME TO EVALUATE

If you've been an adult, or a teenager with a driver's license, for any period of time, you know the places that have long waiting periods. The doctor's office, that popular steakhouse on a Friday night, or even the post office on most occasions. But you know what place seems to always have the longest wait time? The DMV. Some states know it as the DOT. But you know when you have to go here, it's going to take a while.

Every encounter I've ever had with the DMV or DOT has always resulted in a long period of waiting. As I stand in line, inching closer and closer to the people at the counter, I wonder who I'm going to get. Will I get someone frustrated with their day? Will I get someone who is new and a little anxious? Will I get someone friendly? The options are endless.

After waiting in a line that feels like it would never end, you reach a person. You give them your documents and money to update, renew, or replace whatever it is you are trying to deal with in your life. After reaching the counter, your mood may have been affected by the time you waited to get to the person at the counter, so you might not be the pleasant person you were when you first got there. I am guilty of this. I would like to tell you that I am always a bubbly ray of sunshine, but that is just not the case. While I am a very joyful and extroverted person, I have my moments. We all do.

As much as I've pondered the person I would encounter, the truth is, the people working there have asked themselves the same questions. What type of customer is about to come up to my window? Will it be someone who is frustrated that they had to wait in line? Or will it be someone who's a little anxious because they are not familiar with DMV or DOT processes? Maybe it's someone friendly and polite? The options are endless.

Let's think back to Chapter 6. Who is your calling for? Others. Now, let's think back to Chapter 7. What is remembered most about a person? The bad fruit they carry. And what does Chapter 8 say? That God's timing is perfect. We have the ingredients, now let's put them together! Your calling from God will have a waiting season. That is inevitable. But how you wait is important. And how you react to the waiting can impact those you will encounter in your calling.

Here's a question for you: what if the person at the DMV counter was someone that God wanted you to reach as part of your calling? Sounds a little odd, but not really. We will encounter many people in our lives. Our calling is specifically designed for us to reach certain people. No matter where you are, what you do, or when you do it, you will encounter others. That is a fact. There are billions of people in this world. Your calling is to help reach the lost. And there are many lost souls.

How you respond to your waiting season will expose your fruit. As you walk in your calling, you will produce good fruit. Remember, we will go through circumstances that expose the bad fruit we carry, which can impact our good fruit. Here's an example. Waiting is a direct connection to patience. What is patience? A fruit of the spirit. Why do you think God allows us to go through waiting seasons? To produce the fruit of patience in us.

If you find yourself aggravated by the waiting, this exposes the fruit of impatience. Impatience is bad fruit. It is the direct opposite of the good fruit of the spirit that God wants to produce in us, which is patience. A person is remembered most by their bad fruit, which means you have an opportunity to assess the bad fruit, remove and release it. That's easier said than done. What's the takeaway? Your waiting season will expose you.

Let's go back to the DMV. If someone at the counter meets you with bad fruit, meaning you have a negative attitude or are showing impatience, something other than the fruits of the spirit, this is how you will be remembered. That person will reflect on your attitude, your personality, and your actions. This is how they will think about you after their encounter with you. But there is something more important than this: your opportunity to be a light or minister to this person has now been tainted.

What does it mean to be "tainted?"

The Bible tells us that we are to be like trees. If you walk past a tree and see fruit rotting on the tree, are you going to continue analyzing the tree for one piece of good fruit to eat? Probably not. More than likely, you are going to try to locate a tree that has healthy fruit to consume. Your calling is not for you. Neither is the fruit you produce. The fruits of the spirit are directly connected to your character. Your character is who you are. Who you are should be a direct reflection of God. You are made in His image. When someone encounters you and you have poor character, it impacts your ability to encounter them again. It also impacts your ministry.

In the waiting, we must continue to evaluate our fruit. Our fruit that is being produced through our walk with God is not for us. We do not want to produce bad fruit. What does bad fruit do? It makes people sick. God wants us to be a light to the world. He wants us to make disciples of His children. If you carry bad fruit, you are bad for others. This will negatively impact your calling and ability to reach people for the kingdom of God. It will hinder God's ability to use you. If you are ministering to others with bad fruit, it will paint a negative picture of who God is. Yikes!

What should I do in my waiting season?

Assess yourself. While you wait, if
there are feelings or emotions that arise
outside of the fruit God wants to produce in
you, these are bad fruits, so remove and
release them. We want to encounter others
with the good fruit God is producing in us.
We don't want to make people sick; we
want them to feel healthy. We want our fruit
to be a direct reflection of how good our
God is. This is how we fulfill the calling
God placed on our lives. While you wait,
evaluate.

KEEP FUELING THE FLAME

The story of Jesus Christ is the staple
for Christian believers. We know that Christ
died on the cross for our sins to give us
redeeming grace. We now have life with
God because He gave us redemption through

the blood of Jesus. We have been made clean. A new creation. But you know, Jesus wouldn't be here without someone important to his story. That someone is Mary.

Mary is the mother of Jesus. If you don't know the story, I'll give you a brief summary. Mary was a virgin engaged to a man named Joseph. She found favor with God, who sent an angel to tell her that she would become pregnant with the son of God through immaculate conception. The angel confirmed to Joseph that the child Mary was carrying was indeed the son of God, and his name would be Jesus. There is so much more to the story, and I urge you to read it if you haven't. I recommend starting with the book of Matthew.

Mary's story is an incredible testament to her faith in God and her ability to trust in His plan. Could you imagine that being you?

I couldn't! But you know what the Bible doesn't talk about? How Mary felt about her calling. How she walked with God through every stage of pregnancy. What questions she asked or the thoughts she had in the waiting. Pregnancy is 9-10 months. That's a long time.

I can only imagine what questions she might've had:

"What will my baby look like?"
"What will his life be like?"
"Am I really the right mother for the Son of God?"
"Can I do this?"
"Why me, God?"

With every passing day, I'm sure she had loads of questions, thoughts, and feelings. But the Bible does not mention any questions, thoughts, or feelings Mary had during her pregnancy. Nope. Instead, it goes from immaculate conception to her traveling to Bethlehem with her husband Joseph and giving birth in a manger. Fascinating. Do you know why this is? Because your questions, thoughts, and feelings are irrelevant to fulfilling your calling.

Oof. That hurt. It hurt me, too. Here's the thing. God cares about you. He cares about your questions, thoughts, and feelings. He created you with a heart and a brain for a reason. He loves you! God wants you to submit all of these things to Him. This does not mean that He wants them to impact your calling. Don't believe me? Look at the story of Jesus in the Garden of Gethsemane (Matthew 26:36-46).

I want you to think back to every story in the Bible. Do the stories of the Bible focus on all of the questions, thoughts, and feelings every person had about their callings? No. There wouldn't be enough pages in the world to fit all of that in there.

How do you know this is the reason?

Because I've lived it. I've been in a waiting season with questions, thoughts, and feelings. Guess what? I still had to do what God asked me to do, regardless of how I felt at the time. Whether I experienced pain in that season or not. At this point, you've heard a few pieces of my testimony, but this hurts the most to talk about. Probably because it is the most recent. The part of my testimony I never wanted to share, or even go through for that matter. My season of heartbreak.

God moved me to Arizona in 2021, after calling me to move here in 2019. This you already know. What you don't know is how long this move lasted. I was in Arizona for one year before moving back to Oklahoma.

Wait, I could have sworn you just told us you currently lived in Arizona?

I'm so glad you paid attention! Stay with me. In 2022, God asked me to go back to Oklahoma for a year. Then, He wanted me to come back to Arizona. Yes, you read that right. God wanted me to leave Arizona, go back to Oklahoma for exactly one year, and return to Arizona afterwards. You confused? So was I. When God asked me to do this, I didn't want to go. I started planning to stay in Arizona. I didn't tell the school I worked for that I was moving and I began putting money away to make sure I was financially set.

Things started happening in my life that forced me to come back to Oklahoma. Thanks, God! My savings were drained, my health was not doing well, and my job was no longer feasible. Leaving Arizona was now my only option. This was really hard and confusing. I didn't understand why God moved me to a state to have me leave a year later, only to be gone for one year and come right back. So much transition and instability.

"Why, God?"

I didn't know why, but I knew I had to go. I quickly said goodbye to the people I was the closest to. In July 2022, I came back to Oklahoma. It felt exactly as it did before I left. Like I was not where I should be. But God continued to confirm I was exactly where He wanted me. While I was in Oklahoma, God asked me to focus on Bible study, take care of my health, and go to therapy. This was my season of obscurity. A season of being set apart to be alone with God. And as I got stabilized, I fell in love with this season of life.

In December 2022, God asked me to spend New Years Eve in Arizona. He needed me to pray and focus on what life would be like coming back. I was so excited! I got to come home, even though it was just for one night. While I was in town, I saw one of my close friends. This person was someone I genuinely cared for. We built a friendship on our mutual love for God and terrible dad jokes. This person was the first friend I made in Arizona. They had my full trust, which is a rarity. I got to tell them all about life and how I would be back in Arizona in just a few short months. They were just as excited as I was, or so it seemed. It was a great night! So good to be back where I'm supposed to be. Then came 2023.

A little over a month later, February 2023, that friendship abruptly ended. The person I had just seen in Arizona on NYE. The one who knew I was coming back and couldn't wait to see me. One of the only people I felt closest to here was no longer in my life. Their life had transitioned and they

didn't want me around anymore. At least that's
what it felt like. No conversation. No
explanation. Just silence and separation. Much
from myself as I tried to process what exactly
happened. My heart was broken in a way I
have never felt before. I couldn't explain why,
at the time, but I shut down completely. No
more connecting with anyone. This person was
the last connection I had in Arizona. And I was
devastated. Again, there are always two sides
to every story. This is not shared to hurt this
person. I still care deeply for them. These are
my feelings. Losing that friendship made me
contemplate my relationship with God.

That's heavy.

It was. As the months continued on, I
kept doing as God asked me to do. Preparing
to go back to Arizona. But can I be honest
with you? I did not want to do that. No part of
me wanted to come back to a state I would

have to start over in. Not again. And the friendship I lost was with a person who lived here. What if I ran into them? Nope. No part of me wanted any of that either. This was a lot. Too much. And I cried often. Why? Because Oklahoma felt safer than Arizona.

That season of obscurity was so healthy. From evaluating and removing people, places and things from my life to growing my knowledge of the Bible and spending every waking moment with God. It was so peaceful. It was so healing. It was also very painful. But it was exactly what I needed in this season. Even when my heart was broken and I was confused, God was still right there to comfort me. Through every moment. Wiping away every tear. I was good where I was and I definitely did NOT want to come back to Arizona.

God revealed to me the exact statement I made to you before sharing this part of my testimony:

"Your questions, thoughts, and feelings are irrelevant to your calling."

That is not something I wanted to hear. Not a single part of my soul wanted to come back. But I did what God asked me to do. As I loaded up the U-Haul and drove away from my apartment in Oklahoma, it didn't hit me that I was actually coming back until I crossed the state line into Texas. I cried the whole way here. If you don't know, a road trip from Oklahoma to Arizona is a minimum of 15 hours. That's a lot of tears.

My best friend Elizabeth was a witness to this. She knew all about my heartbreak. My lost friendship. My thoughts and feelings about moving back. Liz knew. And you know what she did? She flew to Oklahoma and helped me move back to Arizona. She held me when I cried, she wiped away tears, and she encouraged me to listen to God and walk in my calling. Again, this is why you need the *right* community.

Why did you share all of this with us?

Your questions, thoughts, and feelings are valid. There is absolutely nothing wrong with asking God questions. Trying to understand why things are happening is part of our human nature. The most important thing we need to know is that our questions, thoughts, and feelings cannot keep us from walking in our calling. No matter how broken you may feel God cares about your thoughts and feelings. He cares about you and every question you have. This does not mean He wants these things to keep you from everything He has for you.

To say, I am blessed is an understatement. My job, home, friends, church, health, and everything in between. My life is truly a blessing from God. And I wouldn't have any of it without the season of heartbreak I encountered. You need to know that your heartbreak season will feel like a season of waiting.

As you experience heartbreak, you will wonder if the pain ever stops. Every day, that pain is felt. You may even find yourself uncovering more brokenness from the pain initially inflicted. What does that do? Cause more pain. Seasons of heartbreak are never wanted or desired. We wait for the day we no longer shed tears or feel hurt. And it feels like a lifetime has passed before we can acknowledge what hurt us to begin with.

You know what these seasons do, though? Bring us closer to God. What caused me to contemplate my relationship with God made me evaluate how strong my relationship with Him really was. This person broke my heart, and because they were connected to me through God, it felt like God broke my heart. I couldn't understand why God would let me go through this kind of pain. It wasn't until I truly healed that I could talk about the hurt I experienced. God wanted me to keep fueling the flame.

What does that mean?

As you experience a season of heartbreak, through all of your pain, you have to keep fueling the flame. You are a light to the world. Like a flame burning. To keep shining bright, you have to feed the fire. We do this by reading the Bible, spending time with the Lord, and praying. The same way we build a relationship with

God is the same way we maintain it. To grow stronger and deeper through your calling, you will experience heartbreak.

God is with you in the heartbreak. He saw it happen. He knew it was going to happen. And He knows what He has for you after it happens. To truly move past a season of heartbreak, you have to experiencing healing. Healing means to be healthy. In other words, becoming whole. To heal is to become whole again. Heartbreak leaves you in pieces. God wants to help you heal so you can be whole. Healing takes time. Healing also takes work.

I did not know why I had to move back to Oklahoma for a year. Not until I experienced that heartbreak season. Had I been in Arizona when this happened, I don't know if I would have stayed here. This season exposed my lack of understanding and implementation of healthy attachments and boundaries. There were past hurts from childhood that came back to the surface. Things I had repressed for many years. Had I not experienced this heartbreak, I would not be the healed, whole woman I am today. God knew I needed to be set apart and alone with Him so He could heal me entirely and confirm that Arizona is where I'm supposed to be, regardless of lost relationships.

When we experience heartbreak, we immediately want the pain to stop. We try to consume ourselves with people, places, and things that will distract us and fill the emptiness or brokenness we are currently living with. These are temporary fixes. Worldly solutions. In order to truly heal from something that hurts, you have to allow yourself to feel the feelings, but not let them keep you from walking your path. You have to allow yourself to ask the questions without questioning your calling. You have to submit the pain to God and let Him show you how to heal.

This will take time. This will take patience. There will be moments where you think you have moved on, but something happens that triggers hurt and tears. There will be moments where you feel incomplete or like pieces of you are missing. You will feel like you are experiencing a never-ending cycle or setback every time the pain comes back.

And if we are honest, the person that hurt you may never acknowledge the pain they caused you. They may never apologize or do what is right to rectify their actions. They may never understand or admit how badly they hurt you. And that's okay. It doesn't sound or feel okay at the time, but God saw it happen. He will heal you. He will protect you. And He will restore you.

We cannot focus on our questions, thoughts, and feelings. Yes, they are valid. Yes, you can express them to God. No, they cannot impact your calling. If you have ever experienced a season of heartbreak, just know you are not alone. Every season of heartbreak will look different. No heart breaks the same. And I have been where you are. I have felt similar feelings of hurt and I have some good news for you: you will make it through this.

God is with you in everything you do. Our Bible tells us that He is close to the brokenhearted (Psalm 34:18). He loves you so much that He wants you to heal. He wants you to be whole. And He will walk through that healing with you. The pain will not consume you. You just have to keep fueling the flame.

CHAPTER 12

YOU ARE ENOUGH

By now, I'm sure you think I'm an *expert* at walking with God. The epitome of faith and fulfilling your calling. FALSE. With all the information in this book, I can tell you this: I am nowhere close to that. Do you know who I am? An unqualified vessel. I've said it before and I'll say it forever. Why? There is nothing I have done or will ever do that could possibly earn me the privilege of walking in the calling God has placed on my life and reaping the blessings He continues to give me every day. There are things God called me to a long time ago that I still struggle with doing right now. Obedience, like faith, takes practice. Seeing the fruit of your obedience takes time.

This is the part no one wants to hear. It may take years to see fruit produce in your life. Building a relationship with God, accepting your calling, and being obedient does not automatically mean you are entitled to a blessed life. Some of the things God calls us to will hurt. Pain is part of the process. Pain is part of purpose. We are heirs to the kingdom of God, so we get to share in God's glory. The part we hear less often is that in sharing in God's glory, we also share in His suffering (Romans 8:17-18 NLT). Your calling from God will cost you things. It will hurt sometimes. It won't always make sense. That is part of the mystery that is trusting God.

Here's some good news: you don't have to have a perfect walk to be used by God. No one is perfect. Regardless of what we expect of ourselves, we will never be perfect. There is never a moment when we will reach perfection, nor is there anything we could do to get remotely close. The only thing perfect in our world is God. And only God knows what will happen. He knows what will happen before it happens. He factored in our imperfection when He designed our calling.

It is easy to get discouraged when you are walking with God and don't see fruit. It is easy to blame yourself for things you've done or who you are as being the reason why you are encountering so much pain. Listen, God desires for us to be like trees planted along the riverbanks, bearing fruit in each season. He wants our leaves to never wither, our colors to never change, and for us to prosper in everything we do (Psalm 1:3 NLT). In order for us to be this way, we have to experience pain. Don't forget about pruning season! Pain is part of the process.

You Are Enough

Our God is love. That is the end all be all. Our God loved us so much that He gave us the ultimate blessing of salvation. He sent Jesus to die for us. Jesus went to the cross for you. The version of you that you were before God, the version of you that you are right now, and the version of you that you will become in the future. And there is not a moment that God has ever stopped loving you. He loved you so much that He left the 99 to find you. It's not enough for you to know God. You need to know what He thinks and how He feels about you.

ITS NOT TOO LATE

One of my favorite disciples in the Bible is Peter. Peter was a true ride or die for Jesus. The man literally cut off someone's ear for trying to arrest Jesus. My kind of friend! Peter experienced some pretty significant moments with Jesus. From walking on water to feeding 5000 people with only 5 loaves of bread and 2 fish. He was one of three disciples that got to go further up the mountain with Jesus. He was also used after the death and resurrection of Jesus to further the church and lead one of the most significant ministries of his time.

Before he was able to fulfill his calling in ministry, he had a compromising moment. If you haven't read the story, this is the summarized version. Jesus told Peter there would be a moment in time where he would deny knowing Jesus. He said Peter would deny him three times before the rooster crowd. After Jesus was arrested, Peter was asked three separate times if he knew or was affiliated with Jesus. And guess what? Each time, Peter denied knowing Jesus. After the rooster crowd, Peter remembered Jesus' prophesy, and he wept. If you have never read the story, I encourage you to do so. Start at Mark 14.

Now, if I am Peter, there is no way I would ever think I was capable of this. From having so much faith in Jesus that I am able to walk on water, to denying that I even knew him. There is no way! Yet, this is exactly what happened. Personally, my heart broke for Peter. I can only imagine how much shame overcame him when he heard the rooster crow. How he never saw himself doing something so regretful or hurtful to his Lord and savior.

Have you ever felt this way? Have you ever had a compromising moment in your life that you immediately knew hurt God? That you had instant regret for, but you knew you couldn't take it back? I think every single one of us has. It's at these moments that we feel the most unqualified.

But this moment in Peter's life wasn't meant to shame him. It was meant to redirect him.

There is nothing you have done or will ever do that will disqualify you from God's calling on your life. There is nothing you have done or will ever do that will qualify you for God's calling either. Qualification only comes from God. When God calls you, he qualifies you. God knew you were imperfect and needed salvation. That is why he sent Jesus to the cross. This doesn't mean you have freedom to live outside of God and His parameters and expectations. This means that we have redeeming grace that allows us to continue walking with God, even when we fall short.

Compromise is not something we strive for. If a moment of compromise occurs, take heart, because the blood of Jesus washes you clean. The salvation that we receive gives us the opportunity to repent and come back to

God. To repent is to express regret. To compromise and feel shame is to act selfishly and regret your actions. If your moment of compromise is not something you regret, it is not a moment, it is a choice made out of selfishness. This choice will hinder your relationship with God and your ability to walk with Him.

Why are we talking about compromise? Each and every day, we encounter situations that give us an opportunity to compromise our walk with God. From the music we listen to and shows we watch, to the people we connect to and conversations we have. Our world is full of opportunities to compromise. If you are reading this, and you feel your relationship with God has been hindered due to compromise, there is something you should know: It's not too late.

God knocks on the door of our hearts every day. He waits for you to come back to him. He doesn't keep a record of wrongdoing. He's not waiting to punish you. He just wants to be with you. And He wants you to be with Him. You have the ability to let go of the shame and regret you feel because you have undeserved forgiveness through Jesus Christ. You can repent and come back to God. He loves you. He will always love you.

YOU ARE A MASTERPIECE

Our world struggles with vanity. There is a constant desire to appeal to society's version of what is attractive or beautiful. Social media plays a big part in our lives and fuels these feelings. If you are not careful, you can get lost in scrolling through videos and pictures of others, comparing their looks to your own. We focus on things of physical nature, like being too skinny or too fat. Being too tall or too short. Having too big of a nose or too little of a mouth.

We compare style, size, wealth, status quo, careers, friends, and so much more. All these comparisons have one thing in common. They are all worldly. This is why we are constantly finding flaws in our looks and lifestyle. It's why we buy popular skincare products to remain looking young. We do things like getting Botox fillers and liposuction. It's why we draw on our eyebrows or dye our hair different colors.

Same reason why we feel the need to rush to the store to buy the brand-new limited-edition tumbler cups. Or why we will camp outside of stores for the newest version of a phone or laptop. We need brand name clothing and accessories to feel seen or valued. We never feel like we have enough or are enough. There's a reason for that. Physicality and materialism can only go so far. This world is temporary. The things of this world are temporary. And they will never be enough to satisfy your soul.

We are all longing for a sense of identity. If you lack a sense of identity, you will be incomplete. It will feel like a part of you is missing. To have a sense of identity is to have a sense of who you are. It's to know yourself. Otherwise known as self-awareness. Self-awareness is knowing your motives, character, desires, and feelings. So how do you find out about yourself? You go back to the one who created you. God. If you want to know about how He created you, reread Chapter 1.

God's word explains how He uniquely designed us. He created us from love for love. He calls you a masterpiece (Ephesians

2:10). If the way you view yourself does not match God's view of you, there will always be a missing part of you. Walking with God requires you to spend time with Him. It also requires you to spend time with yourself. To see yourself as God sees you. To speak to yourself the way God speaks to you. To speak about yourself the way God speaks about you. To love yourself the way God loves you.

You are made in His image. Having self-awareness is understanding that your motives, character, desires, and feelings come from God. When you acknowledge yourself as a masterpiece, you acknowledge God as the ultimate artist. Placing your value in God will always confirm your sense of identity. You will never question whether or not you can do the things God called you to. When you find your identity in God, you know *you are enough.*

That's it. That's everything. Before you can be called by God, you must have a relationship with Him. Then, He can call you and you can choose whether or not to accept the call. If you accept the calling He has for you, your first step is obedience. This will require discipline and structure of the calling. You must allow yourself to let go of what is no longer good for you to take your place as a new creation in Christ. To walk in your calling is to walk towards purpose, but your calling is not about you. Everything you've been through plays a role in your calling and when God calls you, He does it in perfect timing.

Walking in your calling, requires you to read your Bible, spend time with the Lord through worship, and pray. Your community matters. And most importantly, *you are enough*. Right where you are, you are enough. No matter what you did this week, you are enough. No matter where you've been or what compromising moment you have experienced, you are enough. The next time you feel the urge to ask, "Why me, God?" Just remember you were made for this. God designed you for this. You can do this. You. Are. Enough.

CHAPTER 13

KNOWLEDGE APPLIED

You've made it to the end. Congratulations! It's been a pleasure walking through understanding the calling God designed for your life with you. Now, here's the hard part: applying what you've learned. It's not enough to know how to walk in your calling, you have to apply that knowledge. When you apply knowledge, you turn it into wisdom. God doesn't just want you to know about your calling and how to walk in it, He wants you to put it into practice. To be a living example.

How do we do this?

First things first, it's time to get closer to God. If you want to know what your calling from God is, you need to set time aside to be with Him. Grow your relationship with Him in a deeper way. Through Bible study, worship, and prayer. As you grow your relationship with God, He will be able to reveal the calling to you. This is where you have a choice. Will you accept the call or walk your own path? Once you choose to accept the call, that's when your life truly starts.

Choosing your calling means that you are choosing to obey what God asks you to do. That's the first step. Doing what He asks. For you to truly be obedient, your calling must have discipline and structure. You need to organize the instructions God gives you, so you don't miss anything. Then, you need to put in the work. Continue to do everything that God asks you to do in walking your path.

As you walk the path of your calling, there will be things you will need to let go of. You will need to break up with shame, guilt, and anything holding you back from God. It will be time for your pruning season. Things that are dead or overgrown will be removed from your life in order for you to produce new growth and fruit. You will start to let go of things that no longer serve you to let God do everything He wants to do through you. Nothing can disqualify you because God has already qualified you.

Embracing your calling means embracing your life as a new creation. Laying down your old life for the life God gave you through salvation. Truly accepting Jesus in your heart and being baptized. The life God has for you is directly connected to His purpose for your life, which is to make disciples of His children. Your calling brings your light to those trapped in darkness. Your calling was designed specifically for you, but it is not about you.

God's calling for your life is directly connected to the people He wants you to encounter. While developing connections to people, we must learn the parameters God has set for us. Every decision made is out of free will. God gives us the choice to walk with Him or walk with the world. Choosing to walk with God is the only way to fulfill your calling. You cannot choose the world and choose God.

Choosing God comes with freedom. We are no longer a slave to sin. We are no longer bound to the world. Our traumatic experiences, past hurt, and pain cannot keep us from God. Every set up is an opportunity for breakthrough. Not even the enemy can stop you, he has already been defeated. To be your best self, you have to choose the freedom God gives you. Salvation was enough to set you free, so live in your freedom.

Always remember that God's timing is perfect. When He calls you, He calls you at exactly the right time. We cannot delay our calling or spend time coasting through life. We must choose to walk in obedience at all times. We can't forget that our calling is not about us. This includes embracing your season of waiting. You will experience waiting seasons in your life. You will also experience seasons of heartbreak. Depending on the type of season you experience, you need to know that there is a reason for the wait. Embrace the waiting and have faith that God will heal you completely and come through on His promises.

Never forget that your relationship with God is your foundation. This means remaining diligent in reading your Bible, spending time with the Lord, and praying about everything. Unstable foundation creates dangerous paths. Prayer is the most important tool we have as humans. Worship is the only thing we can give to God, and in doing this, we show Him love and respect through our admiration for Him. Everything comes back to God.

You are enough. God created you. He designed your calling for you. He knows you. And guess what? He still called you. Everything you have been through, are going through, or will go through is part of your testimony. Your testimony will impact generations to come. But only if you let it. You have a responsibility to understand who God is and what He says about you. It's time to accept your identity as a child of God and walk in the authority He gives you.

Finally, if you take anything away from this, just know that God loves you. He loves every part of you. Even the parts of you that you don't love. The parts of you that you see as flaws, He sees as beauty. Your imperfection is known and embraced. God sees you right where you are. He wants to use you right where you are. Not the version that you think you need to be. Not the version that the world tells you that you should be. Who you are right now. *The real you.*

Your calling is important to God because you are important to God. There will never be enough words to describe how much He loves you. And He has good plans for you. Allow yourself to trust Him. And remember: God chose you.

A Prayer For Your Calling

Prayer is the most powerful tool we have as human beings. It puts our faith into action. When we pray, we acknowledge God's power and authority over our lives, while submitting our current troubles and circumstances to Him. We are opening the door for God to move. Prayer is important, but sometimes we can struggle to know how to start praying. I want to pray with you. Say these words:

"God, I thank you for the opportunity to be in your presence. I love you. Thank you for the beautiful life you have blessed me with. Thank you for the air I am able to breathe and the sacrifice you made for me to have eternal life with you. Right now, I submit my calling to you. It is the calling you have designed for my life. Help me to walk the path you have paved for me. Show me how to be more like you. To bear good fruit. To love others as you love me. God, show

me what my calling is and lead me through the
good plans you designed for me. Help me to
reach those you have called me to reach. In
Jesus name I pray, amen."

CHALLENGE ACCEPTED

Here's an opportunity for you to write your own
prayer. Reflect on what you have read through
this book. Write down what you believe God has
called you to. Make a list. Organize your calling.
Then, write a prayer to the Lord. Be intentional
about what you are praying over. Every detail
counts. Find Bible verses to connect to your
prayer.

Once you have finished writing your prayer, put
it up somewhere. A place you will see it every
day. Actively come back to it. Pray over your
calling often, if not every day. Allow God to
reveal His plans for you. Take time to listen and
obey the Lord.

Scripture References

Knowing the Bible is crucial to your walk with God. While there are many that could be listed, here are scriptures to reference for your calling:

Who is God?
Psalm 86:5
Isaiah 44:6
Colossians 1:16
1 John 4:8
Revelation 22:13

Obedience
Proverbs 19:16
John 14:15
1 Corinthians 14:40
Hebrews 12:11-13
2 John 1:6

Letting Go:
Proverbs 28:13
Matthew 11:28
Romans 8:18
Ephesians 4:31-32
1 Peter 5:7

Being Saved:
Zephaniah 3:17
Mark 16:16
John 3:16
Acts 2:38
Romans 10:9

The Bible:
Psalm 119:105
Isaiah 40:8
John 1:1, 14
Hebrews 4:12
2 Timothy 3:16-17

Purpose and Calling:
Proverbs 16:9
Matthew 6:33
Romans 8:28; 11:29
Phillipians 4:13
1 Timothy 2:4

254

Freedom:
Psalm 118:5
Isaiah 61:1
Acts 13:38-39
2 Corinthians 3:17
Galatians 5:1,13

Faith:
Psalm 33:20-22
Proverbs 3:5-6
Isaiah 41:10
Ephesians 2:8
Hebrews 10:23; 11:1

God's Timing:
Psalm 75:2
Ecclesiastes 3:1
Jeremiah 29:11
Acts 1:7
2 Peter 3:9

Prayer:
Matthew 6:9-15
Matthew 7:7-8
Mark 11:24
John 14:13-14
Phillipians 4:6-7

Worship:
Deuteronomy 10:21
1 Chronicles 16:23-31
Psalm 148:1-14
John 4:23-24
Romans 12:1-2

Waiting:
Psalm 27:14
Psalm 31:14-15
Isaiah 40:31
Lamentations 3:25
Galatians 6:9

What God says about you:
Jeremiah 1:5
Matthew 5:14
John 15:5
2 Corinthians 5:17
Ephesians 2:10

Wisdom:
Psalm 90:12
Proverbs 16:16
Ephesians 5:15-17
Colossians 3:16
James 3:17

*Please use your preferred Bible translation.

ACKNOWLEDGEMENTS

There are not enough pages to truly express my gratitude for every person who has walked beside me during the process of writing this book. From my beautiful family to my amazing friends, I thank you from the bottom of my heart. There are specific individuals who need recognition of their own:

To my dearest friend, and inherited sister, Elizabeth. We have been through a lot in the last few years. A LOT. Thank you for being a safe space for me. For loving me. For welcoming me with open arms. Thank you for always encouraging me to trust God fully and embrace the parts of my calling that terrify me, including writing this book. You, and your incredible family, have been one of the greatest blessings God gave me when He brought me to Arizona, and I love you so all much. I don't know where I would be without you. And I am so glad I never have to find out.

Sharyl, my girl. Where to begin? You are such a treasure. I keep thinking back to when we first met. We were just babies. Now, we are full grown women of God, hallelujah! I didn't even have a home to call my own. And look at all God has done?! He is so cool! But one of the sweetest things God ever did what lead me to you. Without your leadership, wisdom, and friendship, I wouldn't have a book to thank you in. You have truly blessed and changed my life for the better, and I would never have made it without you. There are not enough words in the English language to say thank you. Love you so much!

To the community I have been blessed with at SVCC, I want to say thank you. Isa, your group 'Her Time' changed my life for the better. Walking through so many hardships and valleys, God knew I needed each and every woman in that group, especially you. Thank you for your leadership, mentorship, and for making me feel welcomed and loved in your home. I'm not sure if you will ever see this, but I hope you know you have influenced and changed my life for the better. Thank you for holding me accountable and being the group leader I needed.

Last, but certainly not least, I want to thank Pastor Mike Todd at TC. Without your leadership and wisdom, I would have never learned how to have a relationship with the Lord and truly embrace my calling. My life has been changed forever because of your "yes" to God. You will probably never read this, but I want to acknowledge and honor you anyway. Thank you for teaching the word in a way that allowed me to understand and start fully walking with God. My life is forever changed, and I know I'm not the only one.

ABOUT THE AUTHOR

Emily Michael is a first-time author and music educator. She has devoted her career to teaching music through public and charter schools, as well as privately through ownership of Stanton Music Company. After recently completing her master's degree in music education, Emily aims to focus on bringing holistic music lessons and classes to her community. She strives to serve the community with love and grace, while furthering her relationship with God and answering each call He places on her life.